SON OF THE MORNING SKY

Reflections on the Spirituality of the Earth

Benjamin W. Farley

University Press of America,® Inc.
Lanham • New York • Oxford

Copyright © 1999 by
University Press of America,® Inc.
4720 Boston Way
Lanham, Maryland 20706

12 Hid's Copse Rd.
Cumnor Hill, Oxford OX2 9JJ

Library of Congress Cataloging-in-Publication Data

Farley, Benjamin Wirt.
Son of the morning sky : reflections on the spirituality of the earth /
Benjamin W. Farley
p.   cm.
Includes bibliographical references.
1. Earth—Religious aspects Meditations. 2. Spiritual life Meditations. I. Title.
BL438.2.F37   1999   291.2'12—dc21   99—43433 CIP

ISBN 0-7618-1515-5 (pbk: alk. ppr.)

∞™ The paper used in this publication meets the minimum
requirements of American National Standard for Information
Sciences—Permanence of Paper for Printed Library Materials,
ANSI Z39.48—1984

to

Alice Anne

Contents

Acknowledgements

I wish to acknowledge my gratitude to the following publishers for granting permission to quote from their lists:

Black Elk's prayer to "Great Grandfather," reprinted from *Black Elk Speaks*, by John G. Neihardt, by permission of the University of Nebraska Press. Copyright 1932, 1959, 1972, by John G. Neihardt. Copyright 1961 by John G. Neihardt Trust.

The lines from "Portrait D'Une Femme" are reprinted with permission of New Directions from Ezra Pound's *Personae.* Copyright 1926 by Ezra Pound.

The quoted portions of "The Creation Hymn," "The Hymn to the Aton," and "Hymn to Ishtar" from Pritchard, James B., *The Ancient Near East: An Anthology of Texts and Pictures.* Copyright 1958 by PUP, reprinted by permission of Princeton University Press.

The poem "Turquoise Horse," reprinted with permission from *Meditations With the Navajo*, by Gerald Hausman, Copyright 1987, Bear & Co., Santa Fe, New Mexico USA.

Unless otherwise noted, Scripture quotations are from the New Revised Standard Version Bible, copyright 1989, Division of Christian Education of the National Council of the Churches of Christ in the United States of America; reprinted with permission. All rights reserved.

Preface

For over twenty-five years, I have been a professor of philosophy and religion in a small liberal arts college. I am an ordained clergyman as well. But as time has passed, many of my theological views have changed. Two constants, however, have remained unchanged. The first is a feeling of dependence upon the Infinite, of an awareness of finitude and awe before the Mystery of the universe. "Where can I go from your spirit? Where can I flee from your presence?" (Psalm 139:7) is the way traditional religious consciousness has expressed it. The second is a love for the earth; for its mountains and streams, fauna and flora; for Nature's inimitable capacity to inspire, humble, challenge, and nurture the deepest levels of our human existence, as we ponder the meaning of the same.

Many insights of science, especially those of the naturalists and biologists, along with the noetic visions of Native Americans and the religious traditions of the world, are highly compatible. This is particularly true of those that draw upon the spirituality of the earth, evoking a sense of the sacredness of life. Most of them can be incorporated into a single worldview that deepens our humanness as beings-at-one with the universe, and yet as unique entities, enriched by an inescapable inner dialogue that draws us into the very heart of the universe. This being-at-one with the universe itself, however reified or richly mythologized we have envisioned it to be, is a common thread that runs throughout the world's most ancient traditions and underlies all modern religious and humanist thought.

We change, and our inner self longs to make peace with itself, to return to the elemental. Such a longing is not without a history, or a particular story. And, if we are to live and die fulfilled lives, then we each have to be true to our own story, and bear witness to the truth as we are graced to receive it. It is that truth that I want to explore, as we focus on the phenomenon of the spirituality of the earth, of our underlying interrelatedness to the universe at large, and of that dialogue that invades the very recesses of our thoughts.

Although this book is written for a general reader, it is particularly intended for university and college courses in science and religion, contemporary spirituality, philosophy and religion, and Native American studies. That is a lot to pack into a single book. But we live in a new time, a new era. The "old world" is passing away. A new millennium has dawned. What will shape our self-understanding in the years to come? From a modern viewpoint, reflecting on the spirituality of the earth can help us understand the appeal of some of humankind's most treasured traditions, as well as reassess their value for our time.

The subtitle's emphasis on "reflections" also requires a modest explanation. For the most part, chapters are independent of each other but do follow a biographical and topical sequence. In addition, they are genuine "reflections," not definitive analyses or answers. Hopefully, each will spark insights appropriate to a study of the spirituality of the earth.

Finally, I wish to express a deep note of gratitude to Dr. William F. Junkin, III, Professor of Physics, Erskine College, for his assistance in helping me prepare the manuscript for publication, to Dr. Anne Bowe of Erskine's Mathematics Department for proofreading the text, to Dr. Laine Doggett of the Modern Languages Department for suggestions concerning the French passages, to Messrs. John Kennerly and Fred Guyette of Erskine's McCain Library for locating and acquiring numerous resources, to Alexa Selph, of Atlanta, Georgia, who edited the many first drafts of the earlier versions, to my brother Jack and my two sons John and Bryan, who have shared so many adventures with me, and, above all, to my wife, Alice Anne, whose encouragment and support throb at the soul of this book.

Erskine College, Due West, South Carolina

Part I. Father Sky and Mother Earth

Transcendence and the Spirituality of

the Earth

Chapter 1

Transcendence and Nature: An Introduction

As human beings, we are a combination of spirit and nature, transcendence and earthliness. The modern fields of biology, psychology, religion, and philosophy all share this view. We cannot escape either pole without eroding the depth of our human nature. Take the matter of spirit first. It has to do with our need to put our existence to the question. Putting our existence to the question seems inescapable for most human beings. Philosophers refer to this phenomenon as "transcendence." Zoologists link it to the development of human brains. We have the capacity to transcend ourselves, to reflect on the universe and our life's meaning, and to ask the question: What is it all for?

At the same time, we are part of the earth's biosphere, evolved organisms of nature. We have come from the earth and will return to the earth. As individuals, our conscious episodes are only possible because of the intricate network of physiological and biological processes that sustain us. These in turn are nurtured by a vast field of additional interdependent processes that place us within the context of the whole biotic community. It constitutes a wonder that far exceeds the knowledge of most of us, though we are sufficiently aware of it.

We have come from the earth. We have this remarkable capacity to ponder the mystery of being. That is the crux of the matter. And it has influenced our human development and concepts of self-awareness, at least since the time of our Ice Age ancestors, who traced their wistful bison on damp cave ceilings and marveled at what they achieved.

According to anthropologists, both self and religious forms of consciousness have been evolving for a long time, at least for the past 125,000 years. During that time, much of what humanity has come to endorse about itself and God has sprung primarily from two sources: one *outward*, the other *inward*. The *outward* incorporates the whole grandeur of the universe, of nature itself, or of what ancient man ascribed to Mother Earth and Father Sky. Its themes are compelling and powerful and appear in poetic form in all the major traditions of the earth. The *inward* has to do with our capacity to examine ourselves, our life, our history, and to ask why? Why do we love it? Why do we suffer it? Why are we drawn into dialogue with it? Why can't we shrug it off? Its source is our self-consciousness as well as the phenomenon of transcendence. It is what all shamans, great mystics and theologians, alike, have understood by humanity's penchant to address the universe as if it were encompassed by a Thou, a Living Force, a Great Spirit that will not let us go.

As the years have elapsed, humankind has produced numerous theories of meaning and perfected arcane and sophisticated theologies. From a historical perspective, we are tempted to relativize these. But in their heart of hearts, they represent a universal refinement of our human reflections on the awesome and beneficent qualities of nature and of that elusive Mystery that lies behind the universe and, in age after age, we are drawn to address as a Thou. The rest we have educed from the inescapable silence within ourselves, nurtured by humankind's long story of its encounter with that nameless dimension, which peoples worldwide have cherished and preserved in their unique cultures and traditions.

In the following chapters, my purpose will be to demonstrate the truth of this thesis. First, however, a word about the "spirituality of the earth" is in order, as it represents a phrase that I use from time to time.

Like scores of others, I have always felt close to nature, drawn to what the philosopher Heidegger calls "the voice of Being."[1]   In

---

[1] Throughout the book I return to this phrase. It encompasses far more than nature. Its true dimension is the very ground of all being, of which nature is so compelling a part. Martin Heidegger (1889-1976) was a brilliant

nature, the soul goes one-on-one with the spirit of creation. Its heart is in tune to another voice, to a bonding, that both pervades and transcends the elemental powers of the universe. What is this bonding? this kinship that one feels? Why is it that, after experiencing the "forest primeval," or the roar of its rivers, and the murmur of mountain streams, one so often comes away renewed, becalmed, and even at peace? Both science and religion provide an answer to this question.

Philosophers of religion account for the experience as an occasion of "undifferentiated theism," of the subliminal awareness of the realm of the divine, of being on the threshold of the sacred, of sensing the presence of the Creator himself, insofar as the finite can experience the holy and creative power of the divine.

As a religious phenomenon, the spirituality of the earth is traceable to the earliest traditions of humankind and continues to be mirrored in the beliefs and practices of persons worldwide. In the West, the numinal[2] qualities of the earth are often acknowledged as manifestations of the presence and grandeur of the Creator. In the first century A.D., the Apostle Paul summed up the essence of such theism in his famous dictum: "Ever since the creation of the world his invisible power and deity has been clearly perceived in the things that have been made" (Romans 1:20). A hundred years earlier, the writer of the Wisdom of Solomon captured it with even more eloquence: "For from the greatness and beauty of created things comes a corresponding perception of their Creator" (13:5).

---

contemporary German philosopher whose primary focus was the "problem of Being." In particular, he identified facticity, existence, and fallenness as the three major characteristics of personal beingness (Dasein). Facticity has to do with one's beingness at this particular place and time; existence with the possibilities of one's choices and accountability for them; fallenness with the reality that very few can or will affirm their facticity. Where one does exercise accountability, an "authentic life" is possible; where one flees one's facticity and accountability, an "inauthentic life" follows.

[2] The correct English form is "numinous," but "numinal" captures its essence more powerfully. In Latin, the singular noun is *numen*, its plural, *numina*. The "numinal," therefore, recognizes a plurality of experiences that escape precise definition. These we feel in the presence of the unknown, the ineffable, and even in nature.

In the East, the mystery that permeates the earth is accepted as a reality in itself, endowed with forces and powers that bring harmony and order to the observer. On the American continent, the Native American bears particular witness to the reality of this harmonizing order in his cherished relatedness to all things, and in his powerful identity with "fellow entities." The same holds true for Taoists, and of the strength they gather from the catharsis of meditation and silence, when they have retired to their rustic retreats. Hindus, Buddhists, and Zen practicioners draw a similar strength while meditating in their ashrams and temples, or while bathing in a sacred river or pool. And it is not an uncommon experience for either Jews, Christians, or Moselms, when seeking sanctuary in the mountains or by the sea. Some form of "bonding," some sense of presence, that leads to renewal and self-reflection, almost always occurs.

Modern science, however, offers us a different, but not necessarily incompatible, assessment. From a scientific perspective, the earth's inhabitants and the earth are symbiotically and ecologically interdependent, so much so that we cannot think of ourselves as distinct entities, independent of one another or of the cosmos, without belying the truth of our interconnectedness and humanness. The sparkling debris flung off by the Big Bang throbs in all humankind and in every particle of being. Everything has come from that glowing, magnetic dust cloud and the womb of its creative powers. To see its purple and yellow gases, swollen with electrical charges, drifting in a sea of starlight, as telescopes bring its novea and galaxies into clearer focus, is to journey into its very soul. In other words, the cosmos is in us; we are more than just extensions of its mystery. We are continuing evolving forms of its creative essence.

Complementing this realization is the fact that one's affinity with nature tends to remain constant. Mist and sunrise, sea and sunsets, and treks through quiet forests are what they are. Yet, as natural processes, they evoke profound responses within us. This is true, whether the setting is a landscape of juniper and pinyon pine of the American southwest, the red canyons of Arizona and Utah, the rolling prairie of Montana, or the white birch trees of the north and the cypress swamps of the south. The "voice of Being" speaks to us through these and similar settings, as well as in the thunder of the storm and in the muffled rumble of the surf. And through these contacts with nature, the essence of our human spirit is nudged, nurtured, and driven to question again.

So we are caught in the middle. We have come from the earth and will return to the earth, yet we are capable of putting our existence to the question. Acknowledging, accepting, and celebrating the truth of this reality is what being human is all about. It underlies our religious consciousness, as well as our experience of affinity with nature, and provides the essential grounds for our search for fulfilment and meaning. It is this dual motif, of transcendence and nature, that I wish to pursue in the following pages and clarify to the best of my ability in my *reflections on the spirituality of the earth.*

Chapter 2

A Cosmic Creation Story

According to astrophysicists, our universe was born some 12 to 13 billion years ago. Science's conception of that event is as awe-inspiring and ominous as the earth and sky themselves were to ancient humanity.

Imagine a night of infinite darkness suddenly illumined by a searing, stupendous fireball. White-hot light, silhouetted behind a molten screen of minute particles, bursts into flame, hurtling cores of glowing sub-atomic enegry into the void of space. The explosion's roar rocks the universe and fills it with a brilliant glow. Outward in every direction glistening particles careen. The gigantic incandescence swells, then slowly begins to fade. A temperature of 200,000 million degrees Fahrenheit is reached before the center begins to cool. Rays of radiation and waves of particles continue to race toward the farthest ends of the night. Bands of dust drift amid the twinkling dusk, as the phenomenon of gravity takes hold.

As scientists explain it, it was out of the vortex of this expanding and colliding field of energy that first electrons, then protons and neutrons appeared. From these amorphous building blocks, hydrogen and helium emerged. In time, condensed dust clouds formed, giving rise to galatic spirals of stars. In the process, heavier atoms materialized, such as carbon, iron, silicon, potassium, uranium, and oxygen.

It was in one of these galaxies of interstellar debris that our sun took form, itself encircled by an archipelago of spinning dust. Once more gravitational forces worked their wondrous power and our nine-planet solar system swung into view. Three planets out, a molten mass of magma settled with fireworks into its own orbit. Our earth was born.

In his own fascinating account of this event, Stephen Hawking explains that our galaxy is only one of some hundred thousand million that can be seen, each of which contains some hundred thousand million stars.[3] In addition, our "sun is an ordinary, average-sized, yellow star, near the inner edge of one of the spiral arms."

For several billion years, the earth, its atmosphere, and forming oceans evolved according to the laws of physics and chemistry. Then the earth entered a stage that was favorable for life. In his book, *The Ages of Gaia*, the geophysicist James Lovelock traces the story. He estimates that sometime around 3.6 billion years ago, life began. It would follow a course of three distinct stages.

During the Archean period (3.6 to 2.5 billion years ago), the earth had assembled on its surface those amino acids and nucleosides necessary for the beginning of life. The sun was 30 percent less luminous then, but the climate was sufficient for life's earliest forms. At least, shallow seas were present. Carbon dioxide, water vapor, and ammonia hovered in the atmosphere. Radiation from the sun's spectrum warmed the earth. Traces of hydrogen were also in existence. Volcanic activity spewed more carbon dioxide into the air and floes of iron basalt made their way into the "seas." The first living cells began to appear. They were photosynthesizers and cyanobacteria. They were able to use the energy of sunlight to produce organic materials and oxygen. Slowly, levels of carbon dioxide fell; methane gas all but disappeared. Living organisms began to grow more rapidly. Lakes of ferrous iron formed. They were essential to the next phases, as ferrous iron housed the nitrogren that would replace the carbon dioxide. Through the clouds of transforming gases the sun would have appeared orange, the sky pink, the ocean brown, with pools of green and black bacteria dotting the earth. Reefs of stromatolites, "formed by calcium carbonate secreted by colonies of living cyanobacteria," appeared in the breakers offshore at low tide.[4] Extensive systems of bacteria existed

---

[3] Stephen Hawking, *A Brief History of Time* (New York: Bantam Books, 1990), p. 37.

[4] James Lovelock, *The Ages of Gaia* (New York: W.W. Norton, 1988), p. 85.

everywhere. But of most importance, "all life on Earth was then linked by a slow but precise communication network . . . encoded on low-molecular-weight chains of nucelic acids"--known as DNA.[5] The genetic code was underway. Gradually, the Archean period faded as rising levels of oxygen introduced the next era.

It was during the Middle Ages, or the Proterozoic Age (2.5 to .57 billion years ago) that new cell types appeared. These were the eukaryotes, or cells with nuclei. It was a time when vast evaporite lagoons formed, where salt could crystallize out, allowing for mats of microbiological cells to grow. Their "bodies" created the limestone shelves and cliffs we know today. Both oxic and anoxic ecosystems flourished. The former converted sunlight into chemical energy and produced organic compounds and oxygen from both the water and the carbon dioxide of the atmosphere. The latter were dependent on the cyanobacteria and fed on their dying remains. Lovelock describes the earth of this period: "the sky would have been a paler shade of blue with perhaps less cloud cover. On the beach, the sea would be blue-gray.... Inland, behind the sand dunes and pebbles, the bacterial mats would lie, enlivened by the origin of certain green and golden yellow algae."[6] The earth was ready for its third stage.

Lovelock refers to the Phanerozoic era (0.6 billion years ago to the present age) as the beginning of our own. Larger, soft-bodied cell communities arrived. Plants with roots and stems stood erect. At first small, then larger and larger "consumers" evolved. They roamed the ground, took flight into the air, and populated the seas. The era of evolution, as we popularly know it, began to abound. The genetic code synthesized and preserved even more information. The capacity for self-maintenance, development, replication, and reproduction was now a reality. Organisms enteracted with each other. The forces of evolution, environment, natural selection, climate, and the instinct to survive came together, enriching developing gene pools on a vast scale. Finally, the animal and vegetable kingdoms, and their respective phyla, as we know them today, came into being.

We have come a long way from Aristotle's and Ptolemy's view of our earth as a stationary entity, surrounded by eight spheres of orbiting bodies, and bounded by the fixed stars. On the contrary, ours

---

[5] Ibid., p. 96.
[6] Ibid., p. 126.

is an expanding universe, our galaxy just one of millions, and our sun a twinkling dot amidst the hosts of heaven. Yet it is filled with a wonder that scientists readily avow. Lovelock, himself, is unpersuaded that God exists. For him, the evidence is simply absent. In his view, life would have appeared anyway, given the conditions of earth in our solar system. Nonetheless, he is drawn to think of the earth as the Greek god Gaia--as a living organism, pulsating with energy and beauty. In such a world, "living itself is a religious experience."[7] Creeds only "anesthetize the sense of wonder." In the final analysis, curiosity is our most intimate and human facet of "loving." Lovelock concludes: "Being curious and getting to know the natural world leads to a loving relationship with it."[8]

In a similar manner, Edward O. Wilson, a Harvard biologist, concurs. For him, nature constitutes the "very heart of wonder." We are immersed in that long process of "species diversity," which preceded our own evolution. Consequently, "the living world is the natural domain of the most restless and paradoxical part of the human spirit."[9] Any human exaltation, therefore, cannot lie in our differences from other living beings, but in the fact that in our "knowing them" we "elevate the very concept of life."[10] Even our urge to affiliate with them is in some degree innate. "We are in the fullest sense a biological species and will find little ultimate meaning apart from the remainder of life."[11]

In that sense, both modern and ancient man share a common vision. Whatever the origin of the earth, we are a miraculous fragment of its evolution. Its story is our story. All of its past is encoded in our own mystery of being. For Lovelock and Wilson, no creeds are necessary to celebrate or reinforce its sense of beauty or sacredness in our hearts. It is a matter of living it and respecting it that constitutes our challenge and our call. Yet, the powerful truth of their insights does not negate a religious dimension. The very idea of "relatedness" is itself a product of transcendence that forces us to see ourselves as more

---

[7] Ibid., p. 204.

[8] Ibid., p. 207.

[9] Edward O. Wilson, *Biophilia* (Cambridge: Harvard University Press, 1984), p. 10.

[10] Ibid., p. 22.

[11] Ibid., p. 81.

than mere forms of cosmic energy. It means that we are living witnesses to a *Mystery* beyond mystery that has the power to engender and renew life, especially when our own begins to fade. Certainly, that is the essence of the *spirituality of the earth*, as every theology of "Father Sky" and "Mother Earth" will attest.

Chapter 3

The Appalachian Knobs

Perhaps a brief, autobiographical word is permissible here before examining the spirituality of the earth and the ancient world's cosmologies of Mother Earth and Father Sky. Its relevance will be immediately apparent.

Since childhood, I have always felt close to the earth, drawn especially to the mornings, waking before dawn. That I was reared on a farm in rural Virginia accounts, largely, for the phenomenon.

Our house dated back to the 1800s. Toward the turn of the century, its rough logs were covered with oak boards and painted white. On a sunny day, its roof gleamed with sheets of tin. The cabin's six rooms were large, but its hallways were dark and narrow. They were wallpapered a dingy yellow, amid pale bouquets of pink carnations. My mother, sister, and I slept upstairs in a high-pitched loft. In the winter, it was savagely cold. A cookstove and two fireplaces downstairs provided our only heat. At night, kerosene lamps glowed in the kitchen and parlor.

Our farm lay east of Abingdon, Virginia, and ran along a rocky, red clay ridge, west of the Blue Ridge Mountains. The distant Appalachians rose to our back.

We were of the earth, and as harsh as farm life can be, it sustained and nurtured us. We were a symbiotic community, tilling the soil and caring for lifestock, whose very essence became our own. We were one with the earth, and though we never expressed it that way, our hearts confirmed our kinship with the land in the daily pulse of farm rituals.

In the summer, before dawn, puffs of white mist engauzed the bottoms, and in the evening, the Knobs turned a russet gold. I would climb the steep meadow behind the farm and stare east, toward Mt. Rogers and its hazy range, which loomed mauve in the sun's incandescence. Years later, when I climbed Mt. Rogers for the first time, I understood the magic of the sun's glow. It was early morning and my brother Jack and I were making our way up the mountain's western face. Fog enveloped the summit; the trail was all but obscured. Now and then the mist would lighten, and the rocks and shrubs, lichen and laurel would suddenly loom up softly in front of us. Earth and air, rock and laurel, altitude and summit, were all partners in assisting the sun to create its magical spell.

Sky and soil, wind and trees, rocks and forest have never seemed inanimate to me. The same is true of mountains. As a youth I fell in love with their pine and hardwood forests. As a man, I have never felt alone wandering their trails.

Rhododendron and laurel are another thing, as well as gorges and bogs. Something of the primal fear of the wilderness still clings to them. In my grandmother's stories, thickets and caves were the haunts of catamounts and wolves, lairs where the dark law of nature rules. She made the earth, in all its wonder, seem alive. Wind, streams, groves, soil, ferns, rocks--all were bearers of the same mystery. And we were related to it all. What she felt was transmitted to me.

One might call this a form of animism, of quaint Appalachian folklore. But it is more than animism. At its heart throbs the phenomenon of the spirituality of the earth and the awareness of a remembered past to which we all belong. Anthropologically, we rightfully grasp it when we think of it as a chromosome from our prehistoric past, pulsating in our genetic code, an echo from that time when the forest was our refuge, our hunting trove, and the rivers our source of renewal and life. Indeed, there is great merit to this view, which Wilson himself endorses. There one walked in the "cool of the garden," one-on-one with the Spirit, listening to the voice of Being, as that ancient couple in the Bible did, as they listened to the voice of God. From both a scientific and a religious perspective, the writers of that story were drawing upon an exquisite and universal truth.

Now much of that forest is gone, along with our reverence for soil, and its accompanying biotic community, as Aldo Leopold[12] called it. But our affinity with nature, with that biotic community and its years of evolution, with its grasses and trees, fauna and flora, rock and soil, is bone of our bone. It is the marrow of our humanity. We have come from the earth and will return to the earth, and at death our breath will return to the universe. All of the great traditions of the earth, as well as the wisdom of the earth's elders, share this view.

Our oneness with nature is a truth that even our capacity for transcendence cannot belie. Not even the Bible denies this. As we have seen in Chapter 2, the very elemental forces of the cosmos pulsate in our molecules. They form those fragile building blocks that underlie our long ascent to humanity, that kindle our capacity for action, intellection, courage, wonder, hope, and love. They make it possible for us to be human. They constitute that invisible grid upon which our consciousness of ourselves and our universe emerges and which in turn elicits our reverence for life as well as our manifold questions concerning the nature of our humanness.

Of the things that change, our affinity with nature remains unchanged. And when the world crowds in, experiencing that affinity and its mystery afresh can reawaken our humanity. Why? Because that affinity and relatedness provides not only a passageway for personal and societal renewal, but compels us to ponder afresh the *Mystery* that innervates the very soul of the universe.

---

[12] Leopold died in 1948. He is acknowledged today as one of America's most outstanding naturalists and founders of modern environmental ethics. His *A Sand County Almanac* is an eloquent classic, both for its descriptions of nature and the ecological process, as well as his concern for the conservation of land, fauna, and flora.

Chapter 4

Arcadia and the Homeric Gods

Most of us cannot remember the when or the what concerning our first thoughts of God. There was an old man from the mountains who used to stop by the farmhouse and sip coffee with Granny. He was tall and frail and wore red scarves about his neck. He would sit opposite the cookstove and follow her movements about the kitchen. "Kate, I know that God made you and me, but the thing that puzzles me the most is, who made God?" He would clatter the cup in its saucer and wait for her to reply. Of course, she never did. She was of the earth. And the earth spoke for itself.

I have never forgotten that old man, or his question, or my grandmother's silence. Of course, the cynic would answer that human beings have created God in their own image. And to some extent, that ancient charge possesses merit. But the truth of the matter is that, from this side of eternity, we shall never know the answer to the old man's question. From a purely abstract perspective, if God exists, God is the cause of God's own existence, which is, on reflection, self-evident.

In several of my courses I review the philosophical arguments for the existence of God. I keep them in a folder, tucked away in one of my many file cabinets. I remember once when several colleagues were moving my lecture files from one location to another, Tom Long, who later became a professor of Homiletics at Princeton, was sitting in the back of the truck, when the drawer in which they were filed bounced open. As he leaned forward to pick up the file, its title caught his eye:

"Proofs of the Existence of God." It was all he could do to hug the drawer and keep its contents from spilling. I was driving the truck and could hear him laughing, above the rattle and din. Who needed proof of the existence of God, when the reality of that bumpy journey absorbed our energy?

Homer understood that life is a journey, which, according to G. K. Chesterton, is what the *Odyssey* is all about. It absorbs our vitalities, while simultaneously making them possible. And it is this truth that the ancient cultures mythologized.

By Homer's time, the Greeks possessed a pantheon of gods.[13] Interestingly enough, they were gods of the heavens, gods of the air, and gods of the earth. They were gods of the elemental forces, of the cosmic wonder that underlies all life, facets of the spirituality of the earth. Many of them were gods of human and societal functions necessary to the order and basic goodness of life. Others were gods of those profound and divisive forces that underlie our psychological complexity.

There was Zeus, the sky god, the father of all, the hurler of thunderbolts. Who has not seen him, or his purple robe, behind the storm clouds at night, or heard his crackling lightning bolts strike the earth? Even the poetry of the Bible rings with the noise of this sky god, as he strides across the heavens and shakes the foundations of the earth.

> The voice of the Lord is over the waters, the God of glory thunders....
> The voice of the Lord breaks the cedars; he makes Lebanon skip like a calf....
> The voice of the Lord causes the oaks to whirl, and strips the forest bare (Psalm. 29).

In his hymn of 1833, Robert Grant captured the lightning-swift movements of this Thunder God in his powerful verse:

> His chariots of wrath the deep thunder-clouds form,
> And dark is His path on the wings of the storm.

---

[13] For an overall excellent introduction to the gods of antiquity, see Robert M. Seltzer, *Religions of Antiquity* (New York:Macmillan Pub. Co., 1989).

Even the Koran replicates this storm god's activity, though traces of pantheism have been removed:

> It is Allah who drives the winds that raise the clouds. He spreads them as He will in the heaven and breaks them up, so that you can see the rain falling from their midst. When He sends it down upon His servants they are filled with joy, though before its coming they may have lost all hope.[14]

We meet this god in Hinduism as well. In the *Rig Veda* he comes to us as Indra, God of the storm, and God of the rain. Once again the skies are illumined by his passing:

> Awful and very mighty, causing woe to men, he whets his thunderbolt for sharpness, as a bull....
> And men have faith in Indra, the resplendent One, what time he hurleth down his bolt, his dart of death.[15]

Among Native Americans, his voice reverberates in the rumble of the Thunder Beings, as he cloaks himself in the mystery of darkness and clouds. From the Rockies to the Plains to the Tennessee Valley to the White Mountains of New Hampshire and Maine, Black Feet, Lakota, Cherokee, and Algonquins alike huddle in the safety of tepee and wigwam, cleft and rock, at the approach of his tumultuous, thunderous vanguard.

Then there was Hera, Zeus's wife and the archetype of consummated marriage. She is the goddess of weddings and connubial affection. That marriage should be seen as sacred and dear, even to the gods, strikes us with its ancient and innocent hope for all couples, a longing that we also share. Marriage too is of the earth and of the blending and harmonizing of forces that promote life. The Old Testament may demythologize the idea of heavenly marriage, but not its sacral import. "For this reason a man shall leave his father and mother and cleave unto his wife, and the two shall become one flesh"

---

[14] See *The Koran*, trans. by N.J. Dawood (Middlesex,England: Penguin Books, 1969), p. 191.

[15] See Book I, Hymn 55, *The Hymns of the Rig Veda*, trans. by Ralph T.H. Griffith (Delhi: Motilal Banarasidass, 1976), p. 37.

(Genesis. 2:24). The Koran likewise celebrates the sacredness of this bonding. Even during the holy days of Ramadan, the Fast, the Koran blesses the connubial forces that keep humans human: "lie with your wives ...; they are a comfort to you as you are to them."[16]

Of equal importance to the Greeks were Aphrodite, the goddess of love; Poseidon, the god of the sea; Athena, the goddess of warriors, as well as of women and craftsmen. Wise in her ways, she represents the forces behind organized economic units and peoples. Her symbols were her weapons and the olive tree, the latter a metaphor for cultivation and the arts of peace. That Athens was named for her tells us as much about the Athenians and their self-understanding, as it does her. She too is in the Old Testament in the form of *hokmah*, or wisdom, which God created at the beginning of time and without which human life sinks into chaos.

Of lesser, yet still significant, merit were Ares, the god of war; Artemis, the goddess of animals; Prometheus, the creator of men; Hecate, the goddess of pathways; Gaia, the earth itself; Helios, the sun god, with his fiery chariot that rises each morning, filling the sky with its bright wonder, only to crash into the sea at night. So many gods for so many functions, and so many forces that ripple through life. Even Socrates is reputed to have greeted Helios at sunrise, though he did not worship the sun.

There was a grove of cedars on our farm, on the ridge beside our house. It served as a wind barrier in winter and provided shade in the hot months of summer. Cattle grazed nearby and doves roosted in its green boughs at night. I used to sit on the weathered outcroppings by those trees and listen to the wind in their limbs. It was a tiny island, a piece of Mt. Olympus in arcadia, the abiding place of the elemental gods, a sanctuary for respite and dreams.

We must not think lightly of the Greeks or of their gods, for their spirits and powers lie within us. The forces that make or break life are largely within, even when we conceive of them as transcendent powers. "We Sioux believe that there is something within us that controls us, something like a second person almost," explains John Fire Lame Deer. "We call it *nagi*, what other people might call soul,

---

[16] *Koran*, p. 343.

spirit, or essence. One can't see it, feel it, or taste it, but ... it [is] inside of me."[17]

"The kingdom of God is within you," said Jesus. It is our outlook, our openness to the universe, our sense of will and wonder before its mystery, that contains those resources so vital to a fulfilled life. "All that we are is the result of what we have thought," said the Buddha. "It is founded on our thoughts, it is made up of our thoughts. If a man speaks or acts with an evil thought, pain follows; ... with a pure thought, happiness follows."[18]   The Greeks acknowledged and deified the life forces of nature, of will and wonder, of thought and action. They are inseparable to our fate, or final destiny, too. One does not have to personify, or deify, them; nonetheless, they are present, unavoidable, and inescapable.

In the final analysis, we are all an extension of the mystery of being, and its long history of development and unfolding, in all its myriad forms.   To see ourselves as part of this process, and not as entities distinctly independent of it, can bring great peace and balance to our individual actualizations of life's forces.   Granted, we are self-conscious as no other fellow entities are, but our capacity for self-examination is grounded in the physiological and biological processes that make life possible.

The Old Testament itself acknowledges this, though its authors did everything they could to minimize and demythologize the cultural influences that impacted on the Israelites. For the Israelites, it was the fertility cults of the Mesopotamians and the Canaanites that threatened to swallow up their own culture, more than it was the Greeks. Greek influence would not come until the fourth century B.C. with the emergence of Alexander. Still, theirs is a religion of the earth, a harnessing of the cosmic forces, but in a way that liberates the human spirit and saves it from itself, from its own finite limitations.

The creation of humanity in the "image of God," out of the "dust of the earth," is one of the most profound legacies of the Israelite faith. It unites both the cosmic and the elemental forces in a single system.   Mankind's linkage to the earth is forever celebrated in the

---

[17] John Fire Lame Deer, *Lame Deer: Seeker of Visions* (New York: Pocket Books, 1994), p. 6.

[18] From the *Dhammapada*, quoted in Robert E. Van Voorst, *Anthology of World Scriptures* (New York: Wadsworth Publishing Co., 1997), p. 91.

story of Yahweh's scooping up the *athamah* of the ground, and creating man out of the dust. At the same time, it is deepened by the insight that humanity is more than dust, insofar as mankind has the capacity to reflect on the meaning of its "earthliness." For Yahweh breathed his *ru'ah*, his own breath, into humankind, thus turning man into a living soul. Suddenly, human beings are the product of both the heavenly and the earthly, the infinite and the finite, but a harmony of the cosmic, lived out in a perishable form. Both man's "dignity" and "earthliness" are preserved in the story, as they are in Lame Deer's perception of the *nagi*.

Chapter 5

The Phenomenon of Religion

There is no consensus on how religion began. Entire courses at the college level explore the phenomenon.

Open almost any text you select, and you will find sections on the origin of religion, theories about its evolution and development, informative chapters on primitive religion, animism, totemism, and taboo. Most of these theories are offered by anthropologists and ethnologists and tend to rank religions in terms of stages.

On the basis of this approach, religions are graded on a sliding scale, in which one progresses from the more barbaric and animistic types to the more highly intellectual and morally acceptable forms. One thinks of the Druids, Aztecs, the ancient Moabites, and the cult of Kali, whose devotees perceived the gods and goddesses to revel in gore and require an endless supply of body parts to satiate their appetites, versus the more enlightened Yahweh of the Old Testament, who preferred humility and faith to sacrifice. As David discovered, "A broken and a contrite heart, O God, thou wilt not despise" (Psalm 51:17).

Anyone, however, who has ever attended a snake-handling service in East Tennessee, or witnessed an Oral Roberts healing crusade in a secular arena, or stood in the desert heat of New Mexico to watch Pueblo Indians perform a rain dance, knows that so-called animistic and primitive forms of religion have hardly "evolved" away.

Religion is very much a part of the human experience. It is a phenomenon that constantly grows out of our need to put our existence to the question, as we ponder the mystery of being and interact with the awesome and beneficient qualities of nature. The forms that it takes are immaterial in comparison with the fact that it is a function of our social and cultural environment. Until we finally transcend the need to question our existence, or settle for humanistic values and goals, the greater part of mankind will continue to seek and draw comfort from religious worldviews.

When you pause to analyze the origin of religion, you discover a number of developments that characterize primitive religions and which survive in a surprising array of residual forms in modern religious practices.

For one thing, primitive religion is characterized by an effort to cope with the unknown forces that underlie the universe. Anthropologists have labeled these forces *mana*--an occult power that acts as an impersonal causal agent on all animate and inanimate things. To control, manage, and manipulate *mana* was imperative for early man in order to survive life's crises and challenges. The fetish or talisman came into existence as a "captured" or "replicated" (manufactured) form of *mana* that one could use to control the unseen, occult powers.

For Sir James Frazer (1854-1941), the author of *The Golden Bough*, man's earliest attempts to manipulate *mana* failed. It was this failure of *magic*, in Frazer's estimation, that produced "religion" with its emphasis on appeasing and supplicating "gods" rather than trying to coerce the unknown to do one's biding. In the light of Frazer's analysis, it is easy to think of crosses as talismans, possessing replicated *mana*, and of the petitionary prayers offered within a church's walls as counterparts of primitive humanity's attempt to cope with the unknown. But, as we shall see, the phenomenon of religion is vastly more complex.

Second, primitive religion is characterized by a variety of rituals and rites that provide social and individual benefit. The most famous of these are the rites of intensification and the rites of passage.

The former have to do with intensifying one's relationship with the world of nature and its unseen powers. Various forms of it were practiced by primitive and stone-age man. Ritual dances and chants were performed for a variety of reasons: for ensuring one's chances on a hunt, improving one's foray against an enemy, or creating a closer bond with the occult and elemental spirits.

The bear dance, the rain dance, the sun dance are all forms of rites of intensification. The purpose of each is to identify with the spirits of the heavens and earth in order to assure one's chances of bringing about desired ends. The rites benefit both the individual participant and the larger social unit.

The mass or Lord's Supper, congregational singing, handbell ringers, church choirs, evening prayer services, and fellowship dinners have all been identified as echoes of this ancient phenomenon, from a strictly anthropological point of view.

Rites of passage have to do with human events. They acknowledge that there are critical moments in our human existence when we must move from one stage of life to another. There are biological, psychological, and sociological changes that all of us undergo. Often these passages are fraught with anxiety and fear, ambiguity and misgivings. Rites of passage come into play especially at birth, adolescence, marriage, old age, and death.

These transitional periods still create anxiety for our own era. Our contemporary ways of handling them are not necessarily superior to ancient humankind's. Baptism, confirmation, marriage, and last rites in the church, along with career and vocational training, job placement, divorce, retirement, and death (often in nursing homes), are all modern forms of rites of passage. The last is particularly cruel, and our sensibilities have yet to forge a more humane solution.

Finally, primitive religion embodies a sophisticated social dimension, which historically took a twofold direction. On the one hand, it established an order of priests, shamans, or holy men, whose purpose was to oversee the realm of the occult and to instruct their people in the traditions and taboos of the faith. On the other hand, it led to the phenomenon of totemism, which recognized a society's linkage to the animal kingdom, on whose resources people depended for shelter, sustenance, and life. Totemism fostered responsible ways of relating to the animal world and progressed, in time, to exercise a formidable social function by forbidding the marriage of members within the same clan or tribe. Scholars refer to this practice as "exogamy," or going outside one's clan to find a mate.

In his brilliant work of 1953, *The World's Rim*, Hartley Burr Alexander argues that mankind's religio-spiritual orientation is an inevitable function of his "four-square" physiology: before, behind, left, right; or east, west, north, south. It is this framework, along with humanity's requirement for order, awakened and renewed by the daily rising of the sun, that led mankind to venerate the east and the other cardinal directions. For Alexander, this human phenomenon is primary; all else is derivative.

When you ponder the above, you can see why modern science has no quarrel with humanity's earliest religious inklings, for they have to do with mankind's task of coping with the elemental forces of the universe and his awareness of his symbiotic relationship with his biotic community. It was only as humanity evolved culturally and intellectually that more enlightened views of "God" and of life's forces (the occult, the Tao, and the Holy) began to emerge, which are seen by many to be in conflict with scientific views.

Of mankind's many attempts to fathom this development, none, in my view, has been as incisive as Ludwig Feuerbach's (1804-1872) analysis of the origin of God. For Feuerbach, the idea of God is a projection of mankind's highest ideal of himself. What is man's nature? he asks. Reason, will, and heart. It is the power of thought, will, and love that constitutes the human essence. When you extract human imperfections from these qualities, then you create the abstract world of infinite thought, infinite will, and infinite love. For Feuerbach, this is God in all God's perfect attributes. Thus the divine essence is nothing more than human essence raised to perfection. It was Feuerbach's hope that once mankind realized that God was only a projection of the human essence, the problem of alienation and estrangement from God could be overcome. For, in Feuerbach's mind, human beings are not estranged from God but from themselves. Accordingly, in religion, mankind has deprecated itself, envisioning God as perfect and humanity as weak and evil. Thus human beings have been forced to turn to God to gain back what they have lost in themselves. Religion must, therefore, be overcome. Feuerbach believed that once humanity understood this, then it would recover faith in itself and get on with the task of living.

I have always been fascinated with Feuerbach's approach. So also were Karl Marx and Sigmund Freud. But Paul Tillich, the most brilliant Christian theologian (in my mind) of the twentieth century, disagreed. Tillich was a German-born American theologian, who taught at Harvard, Union Theological Seminary in New York, and the Chicago Divinity School. He died in 1965. For Tillich, the matter is more complicated than Feuerbach perceived. We are driven to faith in God, not because God symbolizes our highest sense of self, but because we cannot escape God, or escape the infinite. The infinite is within. It's not that we invent the infinite and then project it onto the screen of the universe, rather the infinite is an inescapable phenomenon within our self-consciousness. Tillich refers to it as "the ground of being," that mystery from which we have all come and that constitutes an inseparable facet of our general awareness. In that sense, the ground of being is unavoidable. We are all faced with that mystery. It is what the Old Testament psalmist meant when he wrote:

> Where can I go from your spirit? or where can I flee from your presence?
> If I ascend to heaven, you are there; if I make my bed in Sheol, you are there (Psalm. 139: 7-8).

As long as we are required to contemplate the mystery of our being, God will always emerge as that possibility that alone best speaks to the mystery. The problem is, science cannot confirm this possibility, while the Big Bang theory can account for our evolution, our sense of belonging to nature, and our need to work out positive values that enrich the brief years of our human passage. This requires an incredible "courage to be," which many in our time dread to venture, but which must be done.

I. M. Crombie, a contemporary philosopher, offers an analysis of the origin of religious beliefs that is less mystical than Tillich's and more in keeping with the spirit of science. Crombie proposes that religious beliefs owe their inner structure to "two parents" and "a nurse." The "logical mother" is "undifferentiated theism" and the "logical father" "theophanous" occurrences. By *undifferentiated theism*, Crombie includes humanity's sense of "contingency," "moral experience," and "the beauty and order of nature."[19] Contingency recognizes that "we, and the whole world in which we live, derive our being from something outside us."[20] All talk of morality presupposes a

---

[19] From *New Essays in Philosophical Theology*, by A. Flew and A. MacIntyre (New York: Macmillan Publishing Co., 1963), as cited by John Hick in *Classical and Contemporary Readings in the Philosophy of Religion*, 3rd ed. (Englewood Cliffs: Prentice Hall, 1990), p. 377.
[20] Ibid., p. 379.

higher order, or criterion, for distinctions, and the beauty and order of
nature lie all about. All three of these factors tend to nudge humanity
toward transcendence and God. By *theophanous* occurrences, Crombie
means those moments in the history of the human race when certain
individuals felt themselves to be in the presence of God, or interpreted
critical events as being manifestations of the divine. Crombie's "nurse"
is "religious activity." The Christ's embodiment of love as well as his
followers' acts of love undergird humanity's belief in a transcendent,
higher order.

As for my own contact with religion, I owe it to an Aunt
Evelyn, who lived with us on the farm during the Second World War.
Like my father, her husband was overseas; but whereas my father was
stationed in Alaska, Uncle Fred was assigned to a unit in Burma. Since
he was a Catholic, Aunt Evelyn became one, too. She was susceptible
to alcohol, but when she was sober, she was a delightful, mesmerizing
person.

Sometimes I would find her alone, seated at the dining room
table, playing Solitaire. "I'm gonna beat him, honey. Ole King Sol's
met his match." I would pull up a chair and watch her deal the cards
and line them up. The Jack of Spades, the King and Queen of Hearts,
the red diamonds, the black clubs. She would shuffle the deck, rock,
and play cards for hours. Then, she would suddenly break off, slip
upstairs to the living room, and pray through the beads of her rosary.

That was my first real contact with religion. I had been to
Sunday school, but was oblivious to its dimension. It was Aunt
Evelyn's rosary, her need for it, her needing to be left in solitude, to
pray to God or Mary or Jesus, her need for solace, grace, and a purity
beyond human capacity, that impressed me. Of course, I did not grasp
it that way at the time. But I sensed it. I saw it in her face, in her very
being, both in her eyes and in her tears. That we are finite, however
swept with the winds of eternity, of the cosmos, and that that eternity,
that mystery from which we have all come, is approachable, that is
what she taught me. That it actually welcomes us, that is God. That
our whole beingness cannot help but turn toward it. That it is
unavoidable, ever present, ever silent, and always there. That is God.
That part of myself that affirms me when I am lost, that lifts me to
strive again, to dare again, that is God. That fills me with a sense of
power and peace that no "argument" can ever bolster or disprove. It is
that healing Emptiness that I meet in the silence of the self when I have

withdrawn from all else. That is God. It is the *That* with which the Hindu blends under the name of Brahman, or to whom he turns when he offers his prayers to Krishna. It is that thundering solitude that those who have lost all faith in religion hear anew when they walk by the sea, to the sound of Poseidon's sigh.

> Great god! I'd rather be
> A pagan suckled in a creed outworn;
> So might I, standing on this pleasant lea,
> Have glimpses that would make me less forlorn;
> Have sight of Proteus rising from the sea;
> Or hear old Triton blow his wreathed horn.

I love that poem of Wordsworth's, because it recognizes our linkage with nature and our awareness that we are pervaded by forces of beingness, whose presence we cannot deny. My Aunt Evelyn was no exception, nor, in Tillich's mind, are any of us. We are all rooted in that inescapable "ground of being" that puts us to the question, as we ponder the mystery of our own being.

Chapter 6

The Courage to Be

For the Greeks, courage was a cardinal virtue. Wisdom, courage, temperance, justice, these were the classical virtues, requisite for a human life. They are valued in all cultures. Aristotle, in his *Nicomachean Ethics*, lists courage first, followed by self-control. The Lakotas (Sioux Indians) subdivided courage into bravery and endurance. Hemingway defined it as "grace under pressure." Jesus shouldered it in the form of a cross, and after six hours of suffering, died, with his face lifted toward the Infinite: "Father, into your hands I commend my spirit."

As a boy, I remember how frightened I became once when lost in the Knobs. My brother and I had gone in search of firewood, and I had fallen behind. Upon discovering that Jack was nowhere in sight, I became terrified and began running through the brush, whimpering like a young pup. Suddenly, there was Jack, standing in the path, waiting for me. He looked at me as if to say, "Come on, kid, it's time to grow up."

Both my father and one of my favorite uncles were exceptionally brave men. I watched my father one night quietly talk my Aunt Evelyn into handing him a cocked pistol, which she was aiming at his chest. Her eyes were amber with alcohol, her face red. She had been drinking for three days. He never raised his voice. "Evelyn, the gun, please." Finally, she placed it in his hands.

When he died at the age of 85, my younger son and I were seated by his bed. He was too ill to remain at home and had been transferred to the Veterans Hospital in Salem, Virginia. His time was

running out. He had long since made his peace with the Eternal. His
living will requested that, as death approached, no heroic measures were
to be performed. Bryan and I were comforting him, when, like the
dying Christ of old, he said, "I'm thirsty." "What would you like to
drink?" his nurse asked. "A beer," he replied. So she brought him a
can of beer with a straw in it. I held the can while he drank, and Bryan
watched in silence.

It was my Uncle Clark, however, who most embodied the
spirit of courage. He was tall, sandy-haired, fiesty, lean. His cheeks
were always flushed. He wore zip-up boots, loved to troutfish, and was
an excellent marksman. There is a picture of him, in the family album,
shooting clay pigeons. In a tournament, once, he hit twenty-five clays
out of twenty-five shots. He was a true man of the earth. He won the
contest, needless to say.

He was a deputy sheriff, as well as a farmer. I can still see
him strapping a holster to his hip late one rainy night. A fugitive had
escaped jail and had fled toward Uncle Clark's farm. The sheriff had
called and asked him to track the man down and bring him in. The
escapee had killed a man in a brawl, was thought to be armed and
highly dangerous. Uncle Clark checked his pistol, filled the empty
chambers with shells, and replaced it in his holster. He put on his hat,
flashed a casual smile, then walked out of the house into the darkness.
He was often gone like that and kept a pistol in his truck most of the
time.

Uncle Clark's own mentor had been a Captain John.
According to Uncle Clark, Captain John was one of grandfather
Milton's uncles, and had fought with Jackson in the latter's valley
campaigns and later with Longstreet in Tennessee as well as around
Abingdon. After the war, he helped Milton and Granny run a sawmill
along the Holston River. The Captain loved guns, carried them
wherever he went, and raced horses. Uncle Clark's eyes would sparkle
whenever he remembered Captain John, or told of his exploits.

Uncle Clark died in the late sixties. Jack, Jimmy, Frank,
Tommy, Clay and I (all cousins or related by marriage) served as the
pallbearers. We carried his casket with true solemnity and buried him
there at Knollkreg, in the cemetery on the edge of Abingdon. The plot
that I have bought for myself lies just to the south of his. My father's
and mother's lies just beyond.

Courage deepens our humanness and all our other capacities whenever we act with "grace under pressure," or, in Aristotle's words, "do the right thing, for the right reason, in the right manner, at the right time." That takes grace, spirit, tenacity, wisdom, mettle. There has never been a substitute for it. That young Indian braves put themselves to the test is understandable. Without bravery and endurance, their people could not have survived. To appreciate their courage, all one has to do is to read the biographies of those remarkable Indian leaders, such as Temcuseh, Sitting Bull, Crazy Horse, Geronimo, White Antelope, Joseph Brandt, Tsali, and among the women: Sacajawea, Woman Chief, and Running Eagle, to name but a few.

There are many forms of courage, however, and bravery and endurance are but two subdivisions. In the early fifties, Paul Tillich[21] devoted a book to the subject: *The Courage to Be*. For Tillich, our lives are limited by our finite condition, which is characterized by awareness of our finitude, anxiety, the threat of nonbeing, and meaninglessness, for which the only solution is courage. The courage to be. And it has to come from within, from within oneself. No one can take courage for you, or believe for you, or do for you what you alone must do for yourself. And that is accept the mystery of being, in spite of your finitude, anxiety, and fear of meaninglessness. You cannot experience an authentic existence without it. You cannot relie on another's act of faith, belief, strength, or hope. That only results in inauthenticity, or "bad faith," as Sartre would put it. At some point, you and you alone have to affirm the value of life. No one can affirm it for you. And that takes risk, courage. And once it is taken, one is liberated to walk freely in the universe. "For those who want to save their life will lose it, and those who lose their life for the sake of the goodnews .... will save it" (Mark 8:35). What is that "goodnews"? If we interpret the "goodnews" in its broadest, universal sense, at its heart lies the realization that the cosmos is a miraculous given, and every form of life a precious pulsation of value in and of itself, latent with myriad possibilities. "Take courage," the braves cried to each other as

---

[21] Paul Tillich (1886-1965), a German-born Christian theologian whose career brought him to Harvard, Union Theological Seminary in New York, and the Chicago Divinity School. Among his more popular works are *The Dynamics of Faith, The Shaking of the Foundations*, and *The Eternal Now*.

they rode toward glory. "It's a good day to die." Yes. But it is also a good day to live. Well might we say to each other: "Take courage and live. Live out the mystery of beingness that has been given to you."

It is this courage to live out the mystery of being that has been given to us that lies at the soul of both the religious and the non-religious traditions of the world. Almost at will, one can draw upon any of humankind's literary masterpieces and find this theme present.

The Epic of Gilgamesh is often analyzed in terms of a society's quest for immortality and its author's final realization that mortality alone is the human lot. There is an honesty and eloquence about the epic that bestows a sense of integrity upon the Babylonian author who composed it. He, too, had to affirm the worth of existence, shy of any eternal promises of life's worthwhileness. He had to affirm the courage to be, in spite of life's anxiety, finitude, and threat of nonbeing. No god in the epic can do for Gilgamesh what he must do for himself, alone.

In column after column, we watch its hero Gilgamesh seek for a purpose beyond life's journey itself. In the process, he and his friend Enkidu enjoy the prowess of their youth and vigor and achieve a kind of immortality of influence that momentarily quells their anxieties and fear of nonbeing. Enkidu, himself, is a marvelous prototype of the biblical Adam, whose linkage with nature and relatedness to the earth's fauna and flora is likewise sounded. But once Enkidu falls ill, the two heroes know that life is finite and that its meaning can only be affirmed from within, from this side of time. The plant that would save Enkidu is swallowed by a serpent. And in the end, it is the barmaid Siduri who must comfort Gilgamesh with the wisdom of living out his life, not in futility or anger, but in acceptance, grace, and humility.

> Remember always, mighty king, that gods decreed the fates of
> all many years ago. They alone are let to be eternal, while we
> frail humans die as you yourself must someday do. What is
> best for us to do is now sing and dance. Relish warm foods
> and cool drinks. Cherish children to whom your love gives
> life.... Play joyfully with your chosen wife. It is the will of

the gods for you to smile on simple pleasure in the leisure
time of your short days.[22]

There is a dignity about her advice every bit as commendable
as Genesis' own attempt to wrestle with mortality. Indeed, the echo of
The Epic of Gilgamesh can be heard rumbling in the Bible's desultory
lines: "Then the Lord God said, 'See, the man has become like one of
us, knowing good and evil; and now, he might reach out his hand and
take also from the tree of life, and eat, and live forever'--therefore the
Lord God sent him forth from the garden of Eden, to till the ground
from which he was taken" (Genesis 3:22-23).

The *Majjhima Nikaya* retraces the story of the Buddha's search
for enlightenment and the six long years that preceded his final moment
of "awakening." His quest is a study of that human self-testing, to
which so few are willing to give themselves, in pursuit of the "truth."
After an initial year of studying esoteric Brahmin principles, which
struck the young prince as abstract and impractical, he subjected himself
to five years of rigorous ascetic practices, hoping to satisfy his mind's
hunger to know the cause behind human suffering. But in the end, he
found the answer to all his questions only within himself. And like
Gilgamesh, he had to assert from within the will to live out the
mystery of his beingness, without rancor, spite, or resignation.
Instead, he chose to empty himself of all illusions, insofar as possible,
and to accept his life as a manifestation of the mystery of Being that
ennobles all sentient creatures. Thus he became the "Enlightened One,"
the "One who woke up," the Buddha.

To live out the mystery of one's beingness with grace and
humility, vigor and strength, is no small task. The theme is endemic
to every religion, as humanity affirms the worthwhileness of life, in
spite of finitude, anxiety, and the threat of nonbeing. But it is equally
endemic to humankind at large.

In his book *Existentialism* Sartre identifies three characteristics
of a world come of age, in which God no longer plays a central role.
The three are: anguish, forlornness, and despair. But Sartre does not
perceive these as harbingers of a modern pessimism. On the contrary,
each causes us to take stock of the self and assume accountability for

---

[22] *The Epic of Gilgamesh*, verse rendition by D.P. Jackson (Wauconda,
Illinois:Bolchazy-Carducci Publishers, 1992), p.63f.

life. As with Tillich, the only anodyne for overcoming these facets of the human condition is courage. One must look within for a positive life-affirming worldview. To lapse back and re-embrace the traditions of one's past is to manifest *mauvaise foi*, or "bad faith." There can be no satisfaction in a life founded on "bad faith."

In his novel *Nausea* Sartre wrestled with those first, painful, break-away steps that are requisite for a life free of *mauvaise foi*. The story unfolds in the French city of Le Havre, where Roquentin, the novel's protagonist, is depicted as a modern man in search of his being. He too is forlorn, obsessed with anguish, and horrified by the meaninglessness of his own existence. His only reprieve comes from his research, which he pursues at the town's library, and from intense but silent acts of sex, which he enjoys with a waitress, named Françoise. Neither passion nor love accompanies these sexual moments, but they provide mutual affirmation for both Roquentin and Françoise.

One day, however, while seated in a park, Roquentin is seized by an enlightening experience. As he stares at the earth, he notices the gnarled root of a nearby tree. The root is large, grotesque, and twisted. Suddenly, Roquentin recognizes himself in this root. He is starring at the depth of his own being. He is this root in all its stark unpretentiousness and unmasked reality. And acknowledging this truth of self-discovery, as nauseous as it makes him, opens the way for Roquentin to begin that long odyssey toward genuine authenticity.

Sartre aside, no other figure of the twentieth century has borne witness to the need for courage as powerfully as Ernest Hemingway in his *The Old Man and the Sea*.

The story of Santiago's struggle against bad luck, old age, even decrepitude, captures our souls, because we too know that life is a struggle and that at any moment it can be crushed and swept away. Santiago's life-hewn fisherman's skills enable him to hook the great fish, but that is only the beginning of the saga. Having Santiago fight the fish's great strength, against the pull of the sea and the drag of the line, while the old man's hands grow numb and bleed, constitutes Hemingway's way of acknowledging life's stubborn, realistic conditions. He may not use Tillich's words "anxiety," "finitude," and "nonbeing," or Sartre's "anguish," "forlornness," and "despair," but our sensibilities know that these realities are there. Life does require courage, patience, mettle. It also requires honesty, to acknowledge our finitude in knowledge as well as length of days. One cannot escape life's struggles, if one is honest. They have to be met and conquered from within, as Hemingway and Sartre knew. And the outcome? All will turn out well? Not necessarily. In Hemingway's story, the sharks pick the great fish to pieces, leaving only its tattered skeleton lashed to the small boat's hull. And Santiago returns to port. His hands are swollen and his muscles sore. But his spirit has prevailed. Hemingway has given us an example of "grace under pressure" and of a will to live that affirms the greatness and mystery of life.

Yes, take courage and live. It is a good day to live. It is a good day to live out the mystery of one's beingness, in spite of anxiety, finitude, and the threat of nonbeing, anguish, forlornness and nauseous despair, or the stubborn conditions of our human existence. It has always been that way and will always be that way, as long as grass grows, wind blows, and the earth remains a viable biosphere.

Chapter 7

The Flowing Quality of Life

In the fall of 1945, my father, who was a Captain in the army at the time, received a new assignment and was transferred from Staunton, Virginia to Battle Creek, Michigan. There he served as a director of medical supplies for Percy Jones Army Hospital. He would enjoy two additional promotions while at Percy Jones: to Major and Lieutenant Colonel. He would stay for seven years.

Percy Jones was part of Fort Custer, a large army base to the west of Battle Creek. Since my father's people had also been farmers, he too loved the earth. He rented a house for us on a small farm near Fort Custer.

Fort Custer occupied an immense stretch of land, as much as 144 square miles. Like most of Michigan, the fort was dotted with natural lakes and beaver ponds and covered with oak and pine forests. It was a young boy's paradise. Between the ages of ten and seventeen, I virtually lived in those woods and fished its lakes as often as I could. I learned to fly fish in its creeks, catch blue gill in its ponds, and hunted squirrels, ducks, and racoon, from beginning to end of season.

I especially loved the small lakes and wading out into the water to fly cast. Pike, perch, bass, and blue gill could be taken on almost any given day. Standing in the water, with the marsh grass waist-high about my waders, was an adventure in itself. I would flick the fly, or popper-bug, to the edge of the pool, where the fish were spawning, and catch one after the other. Finally the air would grow cool and shadows would begin to form across the water, and the sky would turn a smoky yellow-pink. It was time to break down the rod and go home. I would walk out through the high grass and watch the sunsets grow dark as the reddish-gray orb sank behind the hills. Duck hunts, overcast skies, cold winters, and camping in deep snow were also part of the adventure. But it was the water and being on the water, and sometimes canoeing across it, that brought the most satisfaction.

Years later, when I began studying Taoism and Buddhism, my response to those "water adventures" of the Michigan years made profound sense. Central to Taoism is the experience of the flowing quality of life. You cannot stop it, or pin it down. If you try to, it will overwhelm you, and you will never understand the essence of life.

So much of our Western thought has been an assault on Being, an attempt to penetrate, define, and pin it down, to hold it still long enough to grasp and dogmatize it. But that never works. Life and beingness flow on, bearing them with us. And you have to be part of that movement, that flowingness of being, if your own life is to make sense. "Let it go," is the advice of the East.

There is a Chinese phrase for it: *wu wei*. It means surrender, accepting the flow and givenness of being, of bringing your own life in harmony with it every chance you can. It is the wisdom preserved in Lao-tzu's *The Tao Te Ching*.

> The Tao that can be told is not the eternal Tao.
> The name that can be named is not the eternal name.
> The nameless is the beginning of heaven and earth.
>
> The highest good is like water.
> Water gives life to the ten thousand things and does not strive.
> It flows in places men reject and so is like the Tao.[23]

In his now classic, little book, *The Spirit of Zen*, Alan Watts devoted a chapter to the origin of Zen, in which he grappled with the elusive nature of the "Tao."[24] As Watts knew, there is no single word capable of conveying the true meaning of *Tao*. Although the Chinese

---

[23] See *The Tao Te Ching*, trans. by Gia-Fu Feng and Jane English (New York: Vintage Books, 1972).

[24] Alan Watts, *The Spirit of Zen: A Way of Life, Work, and Art in the Far East* (New York: Grove Press, Inc., 1960), see pp. 35-37.

character for *Tao* signifies "movement" or "rhythm," Watts proposed that writers leave it untranslated. Basically, the thought behind Tao celebrates "the course of nature," or that "perpetual movement of life" that can never "remain still."[25] For Watts, it encapsulates the idea that nothing in the universe is ever perfectly at rest or perfect in itself. "For man clings on to things in the vain hope that they may remain still and perfect."[26]

As for *wu wei*, the concept involves mastering the circumstances of life "without asserting oneself against them."[27] By accepting and adapting to change, one survives change and becomes the stronger for it. For this reason, water symbolizes the highest principle of Taoism. For life is forever flowing, in rhythm, creating and taking on new patterns. There is a Sanskrit word for it, Watts explains. It is *tathata*. It means "just like that." Life is just like that, like the pattern of rain, or the pattern of falling snow, or the shadows of leaves on the forest floor, or the markings in jade.

I remember fishing one morning on the Chattooga River in South Carolina, at the base of the Ellicott Wilderness. It was in midsummer, but the water was still cold. Along the bank, hemlocks stretched their boughs out across the river, and a thin mist formed above the ripples. A slight breeze began to stir, showering the river with tiny, dry hemlock tags. They glistened gold in the morning light. The sound of the river caught my ear, where the rapids turned the water white. I cast my line toward a rock, where I knew that, as the fly floated by, a trout was likely to take it. Just then, the line grew tight, as I watched a streak of pink strike the fly. Playing that fish on the weaving line, at the end of a bent, wobbly rod, and finally netting it absorbed a good two minutes. Throughout that time, I became part of the river, its movement, its sound, the mist, the hemlocks, and the fish. Once I netted it, I removed the hook and released the trout to slip back into the dark water. I fished that way for over an hour, oblivious to any distinctions, other than my consciousness of the act of fishing and the fine art of being, which I experienced as a givenness.

We do not have to be afraid of the East, or of its principle of *wu wei*, or of the Tao, or of that mystery that cannot be named but

---

[25] Ibid.
[26] Ibid.
[27] Ibid.

slips into our consciousnesses at will. The principles of *wu wei* and the Tao is the East's way of acknowledging the biblical story's affirmation of creation "in the image of God." We are living forms of being that owe their existence to a "ground of being" that "gives life to the ten thousand things." It cannot be named, pinned down, dogmatized, or frozen. It sweeps through us and in us and transcends us, and once we surrender to it, accept it, and come to trust and live in harmony with it, we are truly whole again. "He who seeks to save his life will lose it, but he who loses his life for my sake will save it." In the East, this kind of "letting go" is extolled under the symbols of water and of flowing, and finds its strength in Lao-tzu's nameless Tao. How can one ever pin it down?

"I am who I am," Yahweh said to Moses. Moses could not pin God down. That "nameless" power that sweeps through the universe and cradles us and it in its hands cannot be pinned down or confined by humanity. It is in us and around us and pulsates in every molecule, electron, and quasar in the universe; we are throbbing extensions of its mystery. It binds itself to us and us to all sentient creatures, for it is the source of our DNA as well as theirs.

In both the East and the West, the heart of this nameless givenness is grace. It is what it is. It comes to us afresh everyday. It makes no distinctions. It comes to all of us alike. It requires nothing from us in advance. And it is the acceptance of this mystery, this grace, this ground of being, that brings peace and renews commitments to life. As Lao-tzu explains:

> Surrender yourself humbly; then you can be trusted to care for all things.
> Love the world as your own self; then you can truly care for all things.[28]

---

[28] *Tao Te Ching*, Sect. Thirteen.

Chapter 8

The Tao, Zen, and Japanese Gardens

For centuries the Japanese garden has represented the quintessential art form for manifesting the mystery of the Tao and its power to renew life. In essence, the garden is a symbol of the universe and its four primary elements: earth, air, fire, and water. Earth is represented by some form of stone, rock, mound, or pebbles. Fire is symbolized by an iron or stone lantern. Air, so precious to the pre-Socratic philosophers of Milesia, tends to be replaced by plants and fish. Water is represented in either its actual form or in streams of gravel and sand. Both "dry" and "wet" gardens are created to depict the movement of Tao and its calming power.

The paths that lead through the gardens are also symbolic. I have a set of slides that captures this symbolism with stunning power. The paths rarely follow a straight line. Rather, they meander, or stop abruptly, or cross a wooden or stone bridge, or bring one into the shade, where the traveler's next steps are hidden from view. Such is life, the garden proclaims. *Tathata*! It is just like that, as we follow along, from stone to stone, from vista to vista. "Don't be unsettled! Don't be afraid! Come, take the next step!" the path whispers.

Lennox Tierney, an authority on Japanese gardens, explains why the rocks and islands are so important.[29] The rocks represent the earth. They have to be old, weathered, "wrinkled," and have always

---

[29] See *The Seven Principles of Zen*, by Lennox Tierney, Ed.B., M.A., Sogetsu-Ryu Seizan I.

been in the same place--like the earth itself. Islands, on the contrary, represent Nirvana--the place of ultimate rest, the final destiny of the journey (whether across the "sea" of water or down the dry riverbeds of gravel and sand).

It should also be noted that the "sea" represents the Buddhist-Taoist concept of emptiness. It mirrors that timeless beginning, when there was only the void; only endless space, without time or shape, bounds or limits; of that immeasurable time of infinite silence, beyond consciousness, beyond being; the primordial dwelling place of the gods, the eternal *boundlessness* of the soul. To create occasions for bonding with this infinite timelessness is the goal of the garden designer. In Hebrew, its closest cousin is *shalom*, that perfect rest and wholeness that observing the *shabbat* was meant to renew.

The garden also features symbols of happiness and longevity. They are known as "the three friends of the New Year," namely, the pine, the bamboo, and the plum.

Turney lists seven principles of Zen that govern the crafting of Japanese gardens. Each touches on an aspect of life, as it is meant to be lived in harmony with the Tao.

The first of these is *fukinsei*; it represents the asymmetrical. Its meaning is simple. One should not expect life to be symmetrical, for everything to be in order, or neatly positioned between frames. Large and small, narrow and wide, light and shadow balance each other. To capture that in a narrow span of raked gravel, bordered by lichen and boulder-shaped azaleas is the challenge. Standing beside such a garden one can imagine a mountain mist, enshrouding a stretch of moss-covered rock that flanks a rumbling river. Experiencing such a moment can bring balance to a life, caught between joy and sorrow, challenge and retreat.

Kanso is a second principle. It stands for simplicity without gaudiness, for that which is neat, fresh, and clean. Who has not experienced *kanso* when pausing beside a forest trail to marvel at a log mantled with moss, or at a swath of running pine, or patches of partridge berry, so tiny and clean, their beads gleaming like red sapphires amidst a velvet of green? In life its virtue is truthfulness and candor.

Koko repesents austerity, maturity. Everything is reduced to essentials. *Koko* is meant to capture the venerable, the aged, the weathered. In numerous dry gardens, this is achieved by submerging rock under waves of raked gravel, or by having weathered stone appear as worn-down "islands" or "promontories" in the middle of a "sea" or riverbed. Many of Japan's finest gardens feature *koko*, such as the gardens of Kyoto.

A fourth principle is *shizen*. It strives to avoid the artifical. As Tierney explains, "it involves full creative intent, but should not be forced." It is man, assisting nature to reveal its full beauty, without forcing the process. In the West, its contrary rules. All one has to do is visit the gardens of Williamsburg, or the gardens of Versailles, to observe the results of an Age of Reason that believed it could and should control everything, including nature.

Yugen celebrates the shadowy, the subtle, the profound. Most of life is hidden to the observer. No one knows what might happen next. Truth is never more than partially revealed. It cannot be reduced to timeless abstractions. It is never an "it" but always an "encounter." Thus the garden emphasizes shadows and darkness, admidst bursts of sunlight and clarity. This is achieved by arches and doorways, portholes and windows, that reveal only the next "scene," the next room, the next area of the garden and the journey, but nothing more.

Datsuzoku is a sixth theme. It bids us to transcend our worldly attachments, or bondage to laws. There is more to be lived for than society's orders. Compasses and rulers have their place, but they are not meant to dominate the route. Designers achieve this sense of Eastern detachment by creating unexpected surprise. It might come in the form of a tiny, stone pagoda, hardly noticeable at the edge of a bamboo grove, or in the form of a basin of water, complete with a bamboo dipper, at the end of a dark cove.

Last is *seijaku*. It is the embodiment of quietness, calmness, and silence. Just as the Buddha emptied himself in order that life's essential mystery might stir his being, so must the Japanese garden stir the visitor's being, by luring him into his inner calmness and silence where the Tao can work its cathartic transformation. Tranquility, serenity, unpretentiousness, silence--these are mankind's true healers, amid the tumbling flow of life.

From time immemorial, Western man has sought such solitude and transformation. The cave paintings of the Ice Age dwellers more than hint at the human need to hide within the Mother Earth and there express the joy and burden of human existence. So too does David's psalm of 1000 B.C.

> He maketh me to lie down in green pastures;
> He leadeth me beside the still waters;
> He restoreth my soul (Psalm 23:2-3;KJV).

As time passed, Western man moved away from his pastoral origins. He severed his ties with the healing "Tao." He did so largely because of the new emerging philosophical and theological vision of the late classical period. Its roots had already been nurtured in the religious soil of ancient Egypt and celebrated in the Dionysian festivals at the foot of Mount Olympus. Philosophically, from Plato onward, the earth became viewed as purely physical, impermanent, imperfect, and perishable. Theologically, with the triumph of Christianity forward, the City of Man, with its allurements and goals, paled; and the City of God became mankind's highest end and the earth but a realm of transient sojourn. It was a created entitiy to be enjoyed and used, but at death to be cast away, transcended, and abandoned; and possibly, just possibly, if the Stoics were right, reborn out of fire, when "God" created a new heaven and a new earth. Thus crept forward the desacralizaton of the earth and, with it, man's loss of moorings. And mankind became a wanderer in search of a "homeland" that eludes him to this day.

The biologist Edward O. Wilson argues that mankind has forever longed for savanna-like habitats since *Homo erectus* left the African plains. There in that habitat of grasslands, acacias, springs, waterfalls, and rocky overlooks, modern humanity's predecessors moved freely in a pristine paradise that met their basic needs and appealed to their sense of aesthetics. Wilson contents that human beings yearn to retain the peculiar features of their original environment. The fact, therefore, that landscape architects and garden designers prefer savanna-like settings suggests that they are ultimately "responding to a deep genetic memory of mankind's optimal environment."[30]

Seijaku reminds us that that "optimal environment" has moved within. Deep in the silence of the inner self the voice of Being can be heard anew. Withdrawn for a while in the solitude of the garden our affinity with the universe can be reawakened. That Nature has the

---

[30] Edward O. Wilson, *Biophilia* (Cambridge: Harvard University Press, 1984), p. 112.

power to do this is both humbling and ennobling. It witnesses to our unique origin as creatures of dust (*athamah*), endowed with the power to put our existence to the question (*ru'ah*). The Israelite of old credited that "power" to a Thou and expressed it in a song:

> When I look at your heavens, the work of your fingers,
> the moon and the stars that you have established;
> What are human beings that you are mindful of them,
> mortals that you care for them? (Psalm 8:3-4)

Native Americans have endorsed the same path, whether addressing their prayers to the *Wakan Tanka*, the Great Grandfather, *tunkashila*, or the Thunder Beings.

Modern science offers a similar insight, just as "spiritual" and just as profound. By virtue of our common origin, we are all related to each other. The molecular structure of all things is but an echo of the "ground of being," that is itself the "source of the ten thousand things." To accept the mystery of our beingness, to respect it in ourselves and others, and in all of Nature's manifold beings, is to experience not only a profound level of "holiness" and "sacredness," but to be brought face to face with the *Mystery* of Being itself.

Chapter 9

Father Sky and the Solar Star

For ancient man, the phenomenon of the sun provided humanity with its surest linkage to the mystery of being. The sun, with its glorious rays, became the holiest of wonders, symbolizing all the creative and life-sustaining powers requisite for existence. The solar-disc provided the richest "metaphor" for understanding the intricacies of life and one's relatedness to all things. More than just a sky god or a storm god, the celestial sun witnessed to the profoundest mysteries of being that make life possible. The sun brings light, heat, warmth, evaporation, condensation, and growth. Thus it became the visible manifestation of the invisible powers that engender life. Its presence elicited ancient man's highest sense of devotion. It became the window through which the "god of gods" revealed his hiddenness and desire for justice over all the earth. Nowhere is this better seen than in the "Aton theology" that emerged in ancient Egypt during the reign of Amen-hotep IV (1364-1347 B.C.). And nowhere was it given a higher place of honor than in biblical Israel's demythologized monotheism. Both ancient theologies speak to humanity's profound sense of oneness with sky and earth. At the same time, both equally display mankind's awe of the universe and his feeling of being encompassed by a Thou. They represent a spiritualization of our more humanist and biological understandings of our oneness with the evolving universe and our dependence on all its processes.

The "Hymn to the Aton" opens with these inimitable words:

> Thou appearest beautifully on the horizon of heaven,
> Thou living Aton, the beginning of life!
> When thou art risen on the eastern horizon,
> Thou hast filled every land with thy beauty.
> Thou art gracious, great, glistening, and high over every land;
> Thy rays encompass the lands to the limit of all that thou has
> made.[31]

For Amen-hotep IV, the sun is but a metaphor for humanity's relatedness to a mystery that is the source of its "ground of being." Humanity itself is an expression of this larger field of being. It cannot exist without it; and this ground of being is the true force that underlies the sun's own regenerative gifts. Something of the eternal, omnipotent, and sublime dimensions of the universe are, therefore, experienced in the very presence of the sun, whose life-bestowing energies flow into the earth, its creatures, and all humankind. "Thy rays encompass the lands to the limit of all that thou hast made." Rightly did the author of this hymn ascertain man's linkage to, what today we would recognize as, the sun's powerful impact on the evolutionary process. For that process led, in turn, to that long biological revolution in which cells became self-replicating and the atmosphere a suitable womb for sustaining a biosphere. That ancient man should endow it with god-like qualities is quite understandable.

> Though thou art far away, thy rays are on earth;
> Though thou art in their faces, no one knows thy going.[32]

The transcendent and immanent ground of being, which the poet recognizes, also manifests itself in the phenomena of life's intricate polarities: light and darkness, good and evil, life and death. The polarities are inescapable. You cannot have light without darkness, good without evil, hope without fear, life without death. Of necessity, human existence is lived within the bounds of these universal, though finite, conditions. With the eye of his soul, the poet grasps something of the elemental fabric of the cosmos that, expanding in waves of

---

[31] See James. B. Pritchard, *The Ancient Near East* (Princeton: Princeton University Press, 1955), pp.226ff.
[32] Ibid.

energy across an infinite night, remains the bearer of being and its ground of hope.

> When thou settest in the western horizon,
> The land is in darkness, in the manner of death.
> They sleep in a room with heads wrapped up,
> Nor sees one eye the other.
> All their goods which are under their heads might be stolen,
> But they would not perceive it.
> Every lion is come forth from his den;
> creeping things, they sting.
> Darkness is a shroud, and the earth is in stillness,
> For he who made them rests in his horizon.[33]

Mankind is not the only recipient, however, of the energy that flows from the sun. All of the earth's inhabitants enjoy beingness, thanks to the life-bestowing powers of the solar disc. Flora and fauna, plants and beasts, fowl and acquatic life alike, are all vivified by the bursts of cosmic energy that emanate from the solar star. It is a process without end, witnessing to the eternal *ka* (the immortal mystery) of the sacred principle of life. As a result, all sentient creatures are united together as bearers of a common mystery and shareres of a common fate. The author's sense of biological balance foreshadows our own concept of the same. It will appear again in the Genesis story of creation. Writes the poet:

> All beasts are content with their pasturage;
> Trees and plants are flourishing.
> The birds which fly from their nests,
> Their wings are stretched out in praise to thy ka.
> All beasts spring upon their feet.
> Whatever flies and alights,
> They live when thou hast risen for them....
> The fish in the river dart before thy face;
> Thy rays are in the midst of the great green sea.[34]

---

[33] Ibid.
[34] Ibid.

Here is a hymn of creation, sublime for its spiritual eloquence as well as its proto-scientific awareness of the interrelatedness of all entities. Refined theologies of God are only several centuries away, but the birth of such theologies is clearly mirrored in the poet's heart-felt reverence for life, inspired by his awe of the sun.

The poet will go on to extol the Aton for the creation of mankind, the seminal fluid and womb that make human life possible, as well as the mystery of life's "breath." All is attributed to the sole god of the universe, the Aton, the One who makes all life one itself. "O sole god, like whom there is no other.... For eveyone lives, only through thee." In comparison to Homer's chaotic and jealous gods, Amen-hotep IV's "aton" and sense of the cosmos' sacredness is leagues ahead of classical Greek thought. In ancient time, only Isaiah's theology surpasses it. But the principle is apparent. Our highest concepts of the divine have evolved from our affinity with, and dependence upon, the life-bestowing powers of the universe. That we should embrace them as a Thou, humble and grateful before them, reveals something of the highest capacity we possess as humans. And that is our capacity to relate to each other and to all things in our universe as fellow-sister entities, as "relatives," and not just as "things," empty of wonder and soul. It is what makes us human and lies at the heart of our experiences of spiritiualaity as well as our hopes for our planet's future.

Scholars are quick to point out that the Hebrew poetry of Psalm 104 echoes many tenets of this "Aton theology." Fifteen of its thirty-five verses mirror the "Hymn to the Aton." Nonetheless, a thoughtful reading of the psalm reveals the Hebrew poet's care to distinguish between the solar-disc as a symbol of God's presence versus God's transcendent nature above the created order. Nevertheless, the poet's awe for that "order" is the springboard for his philosophical views. And, to that extent, he and the Egyptian poet of the Aton are drawing upon the same source. Listen to the psalmist, as he too lifts his face skyward, toward the sun, its rays, and the billowing clouds, aglow in the hues of sunlight and rain:

> O Lord my God, you are very great.
> You are clothed with honor and majesty,
> wrapped in light as with a garment.
> You stretch out the heavens like a tent,

you set the beams of your chambers on the waters,
you make the clouds your chariot,
you ride on the wings of the wind,
you make the winds your messengers,
fire and flames your ministers (Psalm 104:1-4).

There is an additional facet of the "Aton theology" that also
invites comment. As is well known, the pharaohs of Egypt were
considered incarnations of the god Re, or were looked upon as the god's
"sons." The "Hymn to the Aton" expresses the relationship in this
way:

As thou are Re, thou reachest to the end of the lands;
Thou subduest them for thy beloved son....
Thou art in my heart,
And there is no other that knows thee
Save thy son....
For thou hast made him well-versed in thy plans and in thy
strength.[35]

As God's son, the pharaoh enjoyed Re's blessings and assurances of
immortality but also incurred accountability for the tenure of his reign.
He was expected to rule well and see that *ma'at*, or justice, prevailed
along the Nile. What is of interest to biblical scholars is that, in time,
a form of this theology came to pertain to the Davidic line.   King
David's reign is dated between 1000-961 B.C.   Three-hundred-and-fifty
years had elapsed between the time of Amen-hotep IV's "Hymn to the
Aton" and David's rise to power. It was David's court prophet, Nathan,
who informed David that God had come to him at night and had revealed
his decision to establish David's throne forever and to regard David's
descendants as his "sons." "I will be a father to him, and he shall be a
son to me" (2 Sam. 7:14).   Scarcely two-hundred years later, Isaiah
would embellish this theme to incorporate even higher concepts of
intimacy between God and God's anointed one, the Messiah.

For a child has been born for us, a son given to us;
authority rests upon his shoulders; and he is named
Wonderful Counselor, Mighty God, Everlasting Father,

---

[35] Ibid.

Prince of Peace (Isa. 9:6).

By this juncture, Israel was well on its way toward creating that vision
of messianic hope that Christianity would ascribe to Jesus of Nazareth.
The religious path from awe before the celestial sun to awe before the
Son of God had come full circle. In both a human and scientific sense,
its truth remains inviolable. As Roger Sperry, a Nobel Prize-winning
neurobiologist has written: "The Creator and Creation cannot be
separated. The two of necessity become intimately interfused and
evolve together in a relation of mutual interdependence. Thus, what
destroys, degrades or enhances one does the same to the other."[36] That
humanity should still relate to the cosmic process, its creative mystery,
and the forces behind it as a Thou, and not as an it, mirrors our
essential unity with that mystery. It equally underlies our human quest
for meaning and hope as well as our eternal longing for "peace of soul."

There is a Navajo poem that captures the heart of this mystery
in a brilliant dash of images. It is entitled "Turquoise Horse."

I am the Sun's son.
I sit upon Turquoise Horse
at the opening of the sky.

My horse walks on terrifying hooves
and stands on the upper circle of the rainbow
with a sunbeam in his mouth
for a bridle.

My horse circles all the peoples of the Earth.

Today, I ride on his broad back
and he is mine;
Tomorrow he will belong to another.[37]

---

[36] Cited by D. Susuki and P. Knudtson in *Wisdom of the Elders* (New York:
Bantam Books, 1993), p. 30.
[37] See Gerald Hausman, *Meditations with the Navajo* (Santa Fe, New
Mexico: Bear & Company, 1987), p. 45.

Chapter 10

Art, Religion and Silence

I have always been a child of the dawn, a son of the morning sky. Of that rising solar disc.

Early, one cold morning, my wife Alice Anne and I watched a herd of fifteen deer steal across the back woods of our property near Greenwood, South Carolina. They crept cautiously along the frosty ground, the larger doe pausing periodically to twitch their ears and tails. Then they slipped past the cedars and bounded toward a neighbor's field.

On sunny, winter mornings, I love to sit on the back deck of my house and listen to the woods come alive. They come alive in the sound of a junco's twitter, to the flitter of its wings, to the noise of the tit-mouse, chickadee, and wren.

Far out across the neighbor's field, a hawk circles. Fallen leaves begin to stir; they crinkle in the sun's rays. If you are quiet long enough, you can hear them. A light breeze rattles a beech tree's bleached leaves. A dove's wingbeats erupt near the edge of the woods. I look for the hawk, but all is silent. Even its shadow is gone.

I feel the sun's warmth on my face, as its rays seep through the treetops. I note how the limbs are lifted in interlocking patterns of supplication toward the sky. All around me lies the Mother Earth, robed in her soft mantle of dry grass and brown reeds.

"Great Grandfather," the Lakota prayed. "Mother Earth."

He wasn't praying to sky and soil alone, but to what they portend. To the life giving powers of the universe, which are all given. What his religion taught him is that when we come into the presence of these powers in silence and reverence, with our hearts obedient to the voice of Being, that voice and silence nurtures us and fills us with courage, beauty, strength, and peace. His theology is not far from the Egyptian's openness to the Aton. Nor, in its heart, would it offend the God of Abraham, Isaac, and Jacob, the Creator of the universe.

It is this kind of openness, of quiet waiting, of "emptiness," that the Buddha extolled and practiced, as well as the ancient Israelite. "Be still and know that I am God," the psalmist writes. "Those who wait for me shall not be put to shame" (Isa. 49:23).

In a contemplative vein, art, religion, and silence share a profound kinship.

The philosopher Hegel defined art as a sensuous form of the ideal. All one has to do is stand in the presence of *Venus de Milo*, or behold the *Winged Victory of Samothrace*, or the stained glass windows of the cathedral of Chartres to understand what Hegel meant. For when you do, you know yourself to be in the presence of a sublime power that you inwardly experience--however cultured or of the earth you may be. You feel it as well when you listen to music, whether it is Beethoven's *Fifth Symphony* or Copland's *Appalachian Spring*.

Hegel defined religion as a "pictorial" form of the ideal. The word he used was *Vorstellung*. A *Vorstellung* is a mental image. It is a visual way of talking about what transcends our capacity to grasp in pure conceptual form. It is the way of metaphor, story, parable, icon, image, legend, myth. We must not confuse any of these *Vorstellungen* with the truth itself. As *Vorstellungen*, they help us represent for ourselves what that silent Being of Being forces us to utter in the void of our souls.

In that sense, Jesus, the Buddha, and Lame Deer's *nagi* are *Vorstellungen*. They help us understand, in a visual, pictorial way, something about that Inescapable Ground of Being. They help us listen to its Healing Voice. When Jesus says, "I and the Father are one," he is acknowledging his oneness with the mystery of Being in a way that invites us also to acknowledge our unity with, and dependence upon, that silent mystery, too. So also the Buddha, having emptied himself of the veil of illusions, and seated in meditation, does the same. He too is acknowledging his unity with and dependence upon that Living Silence that innerves all existence, all sentient beings, and that can never be captured in a word. So too, Lame Deer's powerful symbol of the *nagi* celebrates our hidden unity with the Ground of Being. We can only recognize its presence as a Logos become flesh, as a "second person" within us, as an experience of reality that cannot be denied.

It is of further interest that Jesus, the Buddha, and the Plains Indian's understanding of humanity all address suffering. "My God, my God, why have you forsaken me!" cried Jesus. "Into your hands I commend my spirit." Jesus' sense of "Godabandonedness" lies at the heart of our finite experience. What are we to make of the Void? Of this Universe into which we have been born? The Cross reminds us that the Void is not our enemy but our friend. As finite, anxious, and conditioned human beings, we are nonetheless called upon to trust the Ground of Being that meets us in the Void. For there the Being of Being accepts us in spite of our unacceptableness, as Tillich puts it. It is our home. Therefore, we can let go of every life destroying power that would tempt us to save ourselves or manipulate others. That is ultimately what forgiveness is all about. It is the manifestation of grace. The Cross means that, within the history of humankind, an event has occurred that makes it possible for humanity to transcend life's life-destroying powers: whether in the form of fear, guilt, remorse, or meaninglessness. There is a morning beyond all that destroys life. Christianity calls it Easter. It can come to you now. And create a new being.

In a more universal sense, the Cross means that we live for more than ourselves. Thus we require "confession" and "purification" for having pursued less than our highest ends. It means that between what we could become and what we are looms a gulf. Thus heaven bends to earth and wholeness is restored.

There is also another way of putting it. All actions and deeds are irretreivable. Once something is said or done, it cannot be recalled. Once the arrow is released, its flight cannot be stopped, until the arrow comes to rest where it falls. Human actions enhance or curtail both personal and common welfare. The Cross symbolizes the cost that must be borne whenever evil or suffering is caused. We can forgive the causer, and must, but the consequence of our action lives on. The Cross signifies the harrowing truth of this reality. Therefore, we all need grace, as well as need to be merciful toward each other. All hope of justice, as well as any hope of halting further damage to ourselves, society, or our environment requires such acknowledgement and the willingness to forgive, reassess, and press on.

The Buddha took a different route. After years of searching for solace and meaning, the prince Sidhartha Gautama finally came to repose beneath a Bo tree, and there resolved to remain until he received enlightenment. Having witnessed disease, decrepitude, and death, he longed for an answer to suffering. How can we ever surmount life's life-destroying powers? And the answer came in a powerful series of visions, following a self-emptying trance that lasted for seven days. Buddhism refers to these visions as the Four Noble Truths. That suffering is universal. That craving lies at its root. That the cessation of craving alleviates suffering. And that there is a path, which when followed, results in the cessation of craving. It is the East's way of "letting go" of life's life-destroying powers, of finding "purification." And it has brought dignity and hope, beauty and grace to countless lives.

The Plains Indian also understood the need to address suffering. He too offers to God the most precious gift he has--himself. The form of his cross has been the sun dance: *wi wanyang wacipi.* It was and still is the most solemn rite the Lakota celebrate.

As John Fire Lame Deer explains, "it is not an initiation into manhood, or a way to prove one's courage," but "a prayer and a sacrifice."

> Many people do not understand why we do this. They call the
> sun dance barbarous, savage, a bloody superstition. The way
> I look at it our body is the only thing which truly belongs to
> us. What we Indians give of our flesh, our bodies, we are giving of
> the only thing which is ours alone.[38]

Christ's cross, the Buddha's "self-emptying," and the Lakota's *wi wanyang wacipi* universally witness to the mystery of that "Thou," or universal order, that elicits one's most precious possession--the self. All three traditions acknowledge humanity's dependence upon a giveness, a *Wakan Tanka*, without which we would not exist. All three are a pictorial way of bearing witness to the elemental forces and inexplicable powers that have brought us into being, that pervade us,

---

[38] See John Fire Lame Deer and Richard Erdoes, *Lame Deer: Seeker of Visions* (New York: Pocket Books, 1994), p.208.

and to which we shall return. All three are forms of "letting go" that a greater mystery might "take hold" and renew our being.

The Lakota, facing the morning sky "let it go," as he recognized his dependence upon those forces that transcended him, that surrounded him, that nurtured him, and that were within. No one has said it better than Black Elk:

> Hey hey! Hey hey! Hey hey!
> Grandfather, Great Spirit, you have been always, and before
> you no one has been. There is no other one to pray to but you.
> You yourself, everything that you see, everything has been
> made by you. The star nations all over the universe you have
> finished. The four quarters of the earth you have finished. The
> day, and in that day, everything you have finished.
> Grandfather, Great Spirit, lean close to the earth that you may
> hear the voice I send. You towards where the sun goes down,
> behold me; Thunder Beings, behold me! You where the White
> Giant lives in power, behold me! You where the sun shines
> continually, whence come the day-break star and the day, behold
> me! You where the summer lives, behold me! You in the depths
> of the heavens, an eagle power, behold! And you, Mother Earth,
> the only Mother, you who have shown mercy to your children!
> Hear me four quarters of the world--a relative I am! Give me the
> strength to walk the soft earth, a relative to all that is! Give me
> the eyes to see and the strength to understand, that I may be like
> you. With your power only can I face the winds. Great Spirit, my
> Grandfather, all over the earth the faces of living things are all
> alike. With tenderness have these come up out of the ground.
> Look upon these faces of children without number and with
> children in their arms, that they may face the winds and walk the
> good road to the day of quiet. This is my prayer; hear me....
> *Hetchetu aloh!* [39]

---

[39] See John G. Neihardt, *Black Elk Speaks* (Lincoln, Nebraska: University of Nebraska Press, 1988), pp.5-6. Note. There are scholars in the field of Native American studies who question Neihardt's faithfulness to Black Elk's actual words. See *Wisdom of the Elders*, p. 267, fn.1. Neihardt's efforts, however, to be objective and accurate, as detailed in his book's "Introduction" and "Preface," are above question. For further background and commentary, see Raymond J. DeMallie, *The Sixth Grandfather: Black*

We need have no fear either of letting go, as we too face each morning, each rising day-break star, to listen to the voice of Being and offer our reverence to the Great Spirit, or healing silence. "Hey hey, A relative I am. All over the earth the faces of living things are all alike."

Elk's Teachings Given to John G. Neihardt (Lincoln: University of Nebraska Press, 1984).

Chapter 11

Mother Earth and the Daughters of Heaven

The sacredness of the earth has both a masculine and a feminine dimension. The solar star tends to be regarded as male; the earth as female. Yet, in the ancient world, the goddess motif transcended "earthly bounds." References to the goddess were not limited to the earth alone. She was more than the Mother Earth. Goddess worship reached into the starry dome, making her co-equal with her consort husband, e.g., Zeus or Dyaus Pitar, or envisioned her as a matron deity and proud mother of her own divine son, as in the case of Isis and Horus. One cannot read the accounts without realizing that some of Christianity's finest theology about God is traceable to the ancient world's devotion to the Goddess as the true mother, sustainer, and benefactress of life. The feminine dimensions of earth and sky, refulgent with their creative and regenerative powers, are hardly confined to the ancient Near East, however. We meet the phenomenon worldwide. The following six examples illustrate this trend.

First, among the Hopi Indians, a profound sense of relatedness to the earth emerges in their earliest creation stories. According to one Pueblo account, life began underground, deep in the earth. The first two humans were female, sisters. They were given baskets of seeds and images of the animals that they were to help bring forth. But the underworld was dark and crowded and things did not grow well. In time, the sisters poked a hole in the earth's crust and made it into the bright beauty of the sunlight. The spider, the badger, and the locust helped them, forever linking humanity's existence to the animal world. The sisters created the mountains and set boundaries to the four cardinal directions. A mist covered the sisters and one of them gave birth to male twins. The young women married and, thus, began the human race. There are a variety of embellished accounts that augment the above, but all of them celebrate the earth's fragile quality and the fact that humans and all other life-forms are inextricably bound together, across the Mother Earth.[40]

Second, to the Navajo, is the principal role assigned to Changing Woman. Also known as Earth Woman and White Shell Woman, she symbolizes the earth and all its nurturing powers. She is the source of life and the provider of sustenance. In the same way that the earth passes through four seasonal changes, so does Changing Woman. She, too, experiences birth, old age, death, and rebirth. She is symbolized in the soft, gentle shower that brings forth the corn and the desert flowers. She is the hidden psyche of rivers, lakes and mountains. In their puberty rites, Navajo girls "become" Changing Woman and, consequently, the source of future beauty and life.[41]

Third, to the north, the Lakotas inherited stories that equally link them to the mystery of the earth. The stories also account for the Lakota's "redness" and unique qualities as a people. John Fire Lame Deer retells one such story.

Long ago, the prairies were engulfed by a great flood. Its immense waters crushed the earth, turning it upside down. The flesh and bones of the human race sank into the earth, forming a great pool of blood. The blood hardened and after a while turned into red pipestone. In time a rabbit came upon this pool and created a human being from its "blood." Legend names him "Rabbit Boy" and traces Lakota ancestry to him. Still other stories link the pool of blood with the Lakota pipe, so central to their religion. Once, when a member of the Lakota had disappeared, they found his "remains" and the tribe's pipe at the foot of a hill, near the red pipestone rock. Realizing he was dead, the tribe prayed for him. As one man prayed, he leaned his head against the rock and, from deep within the earth, heard this voice: "This is my blood, which you are going to use." Lame Deer goes on to link

---

[40] See *Wisdom of the Elders*, pp. 32-33.
[41] See Hausman's discussion of Changing Woman, op. cit., pp. 13-16. For a more thorough investigation, see Raymond Friday Locke's *The Book of the Navajo* (Los Angles: Mankind Publishing Co., 1992).

the redness of the Indian with the pipestone and offers this exquisite insight:

> As we stand on grandmother earth, raising our sacred pipe in prayer, its stem forms a bridge from earth through man through our bodies, to the sky, to Wakan Tanka, the grandfather spirit. As the pipe is filled with our sacred red willow bark tobacco, each tiny grain represents one of the living things on this earth. All of the Great Spirit's creations, the whole universe, is in the pipe. All of us is in that pipe at the moment of prayer.... This pipe is our most sacred possession.[42]

    In separate works, both Black Elk and Lame Deer preserve the legend of the White Calf Buffalo Woman and her gift of the pipe to the Lakota people. Her role in "humanizing" the Lakotas is unparalleled, although there are similarities between her gifts and activities and those of White Shell Woman. The operative principle at the heart of the Buffalo Woman story, however, has to do with the sacredness of the earth and the Lakota's unity with all living things. In particular, it hallows the Lakota relatedness to the prairie, the Black Hills, the buffalo, the sky, the winds, and the cycles of life that time had established on the Plains. This "goddess of the prairie," come down from heaven, is the Lakota's true "ground of being," providing order, grace, and direction throughout their lives.

    In Black Elk's version, two scouts were searching for bison. Climbing a hill, they saw in the distance a beautiful young woman coming toward them. She was dressed in white buckskin. One of the scouts became enflamed with lust and rode out to meet her. He never returned. After he disappeared in a veil of mist, the woman ordered the remaining scout to return to his people and prepare for her arrival. She approached the tribal chiefs, as a song on the wind, as they awaited her inside their council tepee. She gave them the pipe. A bison calf was carved on one side, representing the earth and its animals that sustained them; twelve eagle feathers hung from its stem, representing the lunar year and the cycles of time. The feathers were tied together with a "grass that never breaks." Then she spoke: "With this you shall multiply and be a good nation. Nothing but good shall come from it.

---

[42] op. cit. p. 264.

Only the hands of the good shall take care of it and the bad shall not even see it." Just before departing, she sang again, left the tepee, and suddenly turned into a white buffalo and galloped away.[43]

Both my Aunt Evelyn and Uncle Clark had pronounced cheekbones. Their skin was clear and fair but would take on a reddish hue if either were piqued or put on the defensive. My grandmother's people hailed from deep in the Knobs. Her hair was long and straight, though she kept it in a bun. Her love for the earth, for wind and sky, and all living things has made me wonder if she wasn't descended from the Cherokees or even the Shawnee, who roamed Virginia's forests before being repulsed into Kentucky. My brother loves to tell of an Indian brave whose raiding parties terrorized the Virginia frontier of the late 1700s. The brave was big, strong, and fearless. He could outrun a man on a horse, drag him down and kill him before the terrified victim could reach for a knife. On many of his raiding parties he assuaged his anger by kidnapping frontier women and taking them back to Ohio. Could my grandmother's great-great-grandmother have been one of those hapless girls, who eventually slipped her way back across the mountains to her cherished Knobs, carrying her infant son or daughter in her arms?

Whatever the case, since reading Lame Deer's account of the red pipestone, I have acquired a new appreciation for the earth of the Knobs. The soil of mountainous Virginia, the Carolina Piedmont, the valleys of Tennessee, and much of northern Georgia and Alabama is red. Rich in iron and silicates, this red clay pan stretches across most of the South's uplands. It is there for all to see. How I used to bemoan it as a child when it stuck between my bare toes like a red glue. It was inescapable. Yet, it has become a bridge now for something far more profound. Anyone from such a soil can cherish his or her linkage with the mystery of Being, the Mother Earth, and all one's fellow-sister neighbors. The phrase "red or yellow, black or white" takes on a new meaning when the pigments are associated, not simply with skin, but with the very essence of the earth's soils, mother to all.

The fourth example returns us to the ancient Near East, to Mesopotamia, and to the goddess Ishtar. Here the feminine principle became a transparent symbol for co-equality with God. Ishtar represents far more than the passive, receptive, fecund earth. The planet Venus,

---

[43] *Black Elk Speaks*, pp. 3-5.

the Morning Star, became her image-form. With her, we are elevated to the chambers of the gods, to the daughters of heaven. Indeed, she is the queen of all. As the Mother Goddess, her ways are co-equal with the godhead, with eternity, wisdom, love, life, and providence. All of the qualities of divinity, eternity, wisdom, omniscience, love, creative power, and the sole right to determine human fate are attributed to her. All one has to do is read the "Hymn to Ishtar" to discover them. Here is a sampling of the attributes assigned to her:

> Praise Ishtar, the most awesome of the goddesses.
> She is clothed with pleasure and love.
> She is laden with vitality, charm, and voluptuousness.
>
> In lips she is sweet; life is in her mouth....
> Her figure is beautiful; her eyes are brilliant.
>
> The goddess--with her there is counsel.
> The fate of everything she holds in her hand.
> At her glance there is created joy,
> Power, magnificence, the protecting deity and guardian spirit.
>
> Ishtar--to her greatness who can be equal?
> Strong, exalted, splendid are her decrees.
>
> She is sought after among the gods; extraordinary is her station.
> Respected is her word; it is supreme over them.
>
> She is their queen; they continually cause her commands to be executed.
> All of them bow down before her.

Then of the king whose kingdom worships her the Hymn concludes:

> By her orders she has subjected to him
> four world regions at his feet;
> And the total of all peoples
> She has decided to attach them to his yoke.[44]

---

[44] Pritchard, pp. 232f.

Of the many things that could be noted, observe the emphasis on her decrees, counsel, and commands. She is the embodiment of wisdom; hers is the highest way of the universe. Her vision is supreme. Anthropologists remind us that the earliest periods of the Neolithic era were matrilineal. This was especially true throughout the ancient Near East, where the Mother Goddess reigned supreme. It was only after the invasions of the Northern Indo-Aryans that the feminine principle became subject to male revision and censure. All across the ancient Near East, the male principle came to dominate. Consequently, wisdom became a "consort" of God, rather than God's true equal. Human fate was taken from the Goddess's hands, and male gods decreed mankind's limits. This is especially the case in *The Epic of Gilgamesh*, where, following the flood, the brooding gods (all male) quarrel among themselves and elevate Utnapishtim to immortality but assign mortality to the rest of humankind.

This brings us to the fifth example, the Bible, and its use of the feminine principle as well as its "downsizing" of the same. In Hebrew, the words *ru'ah* (wind, breath, spirit) and *athamah* (soil, ground) are feminine. The latter is the passive, fecund source upon which the male god Yahweh Elohim plies his creative power. In the Genesis story, the feminine principle (*athamah*) becomes the veritable "soil" out of which *Atham*, Adam, is born. God breathes his *ru'ah* into the *athamah*, but note that the *ru'ah* (feminine) is now part of God's very beingness. It is no longer an independent, free "spirit," separate, and co-equal with God.

Of further interest is what happens to "wisdom." In the "Hymn to Ishtar," the Mother Goddess embodies wisdom. Her decrees and commands are executed by the gods themselves. But in the Old Testament, wisdom, or *hokmah* (feminine), becomes a "daughter" of God. Nonetheless, in spite of her subordination to God, *hokmah* receives an honor as supreme as any accorded Ishtar. The tradition was too revered to deny the influence that ancient goddess worship had had on the ancestors of the Hebrew people. Proverbs 8 preserves that ancient connection with remarkable transparency.

> The Lord created me at the beginning of his work, the first of
> his acts of long ago....
> Before the mountains had been shaped, before the hills, I was
> brought forth--

When he had not yet made earth and fields....
I was beside him, like a master worker; and I was daily his
delight, rejoicing before him always, rejoicing in his inhabited
world and delighting in the human race.
And now, my children, listen to me: happy are those who keep
my ways.
By me kings reign, and rulers decree what is just; by me rulers
rule,... and all who govern rightly (vss. 22,25,30-32,15-16).

An additional nuance is also detectable in the Israelite
promotion of Father Sky over Mother Earth forces. The feminine
elements of soil, breath, wind, mist, and wisdom witness to that earlier
timeframe when matrilineal cultures dominated the Fertile Crescent.
When those societies later succumbed to the emerging nomadic warrior
cultures, feminine gods were suppressed in favor of male hero deities,
such as Anu, Ea, Shamash, and Marduk of the Babylonian myths. In
Israel, a blending would occur, in which all the creative and cosmic
powers were united and attributed to the will and activity of Yahweh
alone.

Even more remarkable is the fact that the first five books of
the Bible are known as the Torah--the teaching, the law. The word
Torah is also feminine. The Torah constitutes the heart of Judaism's
most cherished precepts, stories, and sagas. It is the repository of a
legacy that reaches back to the phenomenon of human awe both before
the trembling heavens above, bright with the morning star, and the
mystery of the earth's capacity to generate life. Here, the spirituality of
earth and sky, heaven and soil, bond together to inspire a sense of
devotion and wonder that has created one of the most enduring religious
visions of mankind. Far from being in conflict with science, this
poetic view of the universe affirms that we are genuinely a true
extension of all those galatic powers, pregnant with vitality and
potential, flung out by the Big Bang and the Mystery behind it.
Learning to fathom its "decrees" and "commands" and learning "to keep
them" indeed points the way to wisdom: for ourselves, our progeny, and
all the earth's holy beings. And that our hearts are drawn to utter a
"Thou" only deepens our humanity and sense of relatedness, not only to
all things, but to that very Mystery itself. It is like sending a song, a
poem, a refrain, across the universe in gratitude for our being here.

Which is what the old legends and hymns to the Aton and Ishtar were all about.[45]

Our final example takes us to India and to the ancient goddess Dawn. Like *hokmah*, she is a daughter of heaven; like Ishtar, she is the goddess of supreme attributes. In the *Rig Veda*, that ancient prayerbook of the Hindus, hymn after hymn praises Dawn for her boundless acts of felicity and providential kindness toward humankind. She is the Lady of Light, the Daughter of the Sky, the Daughter of Heaven. Her sister is Darkness, but she is the Dawn, the new day. She is the protectress of all, the dispeller of darkness, and causes her light to shine on everyone, alike. She is immortal, imperishable, omniscient. She renews life's daily resources and bestows life's blessings and bounty on all who truly worship her. Immune to the acids of time, she measures out humanity's finitude and grant's life's fortune "to all the race of mortals." But above all, she is the protectress of the Law, of the "path of Order" itself. For in the act of her daily rising and her glorious red appearance each morning, she mirrors the higher universal orders, hidden from mankind, but observable in her perpetual routine. Thus, her arrival awakens her devotees to the higher moral and natural laws, by which all humanity and sentient beings are meant to live. Perhaps this one citation is sufficient:

> This light is come, amid all lights the fairest....
> All living creatures hath the Dawn awakened.
> One to high sway, one to exalted glory,
> one to pursue his gain, and one his labour.
> All to regard their different vocations, all moving creatures
> hath the Dawn awakened....
> From days eternal hath Dawn shone, the Goddess,....
> So will she shine on days to come; immortal she moves on in
> her own strength, undecaying....
> Bringing all life-sustaining blessings with her, showing
> herself she sends forth brilliant lustre.[46]

The phenomenon of the Earth as a mother and the awareness of an "ordering" principle at work in the universe inspired antiquity to

---

[45] For more information on the role of goddess worship, see chap. 3 in *Religions of Antiquity*.

[46] *The Rig Veda*, Book I, Hymn 113.

create mother goddesses as the only adequate response to the mystery of Being. To that extent, ancient man's sense of relatedness to Being was enhanced by his "spiritual" interpretation of the celestial and terrestrial orders as embodying feminine qualities. That led to a sense of reverence for the cosmos and deepened both his respect for and acknowledged dependence on all its powers and resources.

By way of addendum, few contemporary writers can improve on Marilou Awiakta's interpretation of this principle. In her book *Selu: Seeking the Corn-Mother's Wisdom*, Awiakta retells the Cherokee myth of the Corn-Mother and explores its meaning for a modern world.

There are several versions of the story. Perhaps the oldest in print is that found in James Mooney's *History, Myths, and Sacred Formulas of the Cherokee.*

According to legend, the first couple were Kanati and Selu. Kanati was a great hunter and provided for his wife Selu and their two sons with ample game from the mountains. Kanati knew of a secret place, hidden behind a rock, where animals lived, and rolling the rock to one side, he'd release only enough game to keep his family supplied. The boys discovered this secret place, and, rolling the rock aside, watched helplessly as all the animals escaped.

When the boys returned home, they were hungry. "Wait here," their mother said, "and I will get you something to eat." She left the cabin and entered a storehouse. The boys followed and spied on her through the building's cracks. Inside the storeroom, Selu set a basket under her and rubbing, first her stomach and then under her arms, filled the basket with corn. "She's a witch," the boys concluded. "We'll have to kill her."

When Selu emerged from the storehouse, she read their eyes. "After you kill me," she said, "you must clear some ground in front of the cabin. Drag my body around it seven times, then seven more times within the circle. Keep watch all night and in the morning you will have plenty of corn to eat." The boys killed her, but after clearing the ground, they dragged her body only over seven spots, and then only twice within the circle.

As Awiakta explains, the legend has to do with far more than a simple myth about origins, or why the Cherokee only work their corn twice. It has to do with respect, with reverence for the earth, with its hidden law that the Creator has placed within it: "If you take from the earth, you must put something back." It is a sacred law, for it has to do with the highest kind of reverence that sustains life and keeps it in balance.

If you take from Nature, you must put something back.

If you take from your parents, your spouse, your children, your loved ones, your neighbors, your country, you must give something back.

Above all, if you take from the Holy, the Eternal, the Sacred, the Creator, the Giver, God, or even the Mystery beyond God, you must give something back. Your self. Your heart. Your mind. Your strength. Respect. Reverence. Action. Justice. Kindness. Mercy. Love.

Chapter 12

Sexual Love: Earth's Gracious Gift to Humanity

No overview of earth's spirituality would be complete if it failed to acknowledge mankind's awe of sex. Of all the things the Queen of Heaven symbolized, her gift of sex ranks at the top. That it was cherished and held sacred is mirrored in all the goddess cults of the ancient Near East. In Hinduism, it is yoked with the phenomenon of *shakti*, an aspect of the universe's energy flow. Among Navajos, as we have seen, the gifts of love and sex were apotheosized in the legends of Changing Woman--the goddess of puberty, women, beauty, and reproduction. For Cherokees, the sacredness of the human balance is preserved in the stories of Selu and Kanati, the archetypal couple that unite humanity's most powerful forces. For Israel, it is the gift of God himself, who bestows the deepest levels of human intimacy for humankind to enjoy.

Love and sex and the human drive to enjoy, protect, and even control them continues to undergo an extraordinary history. Over the face of time, our attitudes have ranged from openness and acceptance to prudish and coercive measures to shame any and all who deviate from the defined norm. That the religious basis for the Victorian code has eroded in our time partially explains why a new era of "promiscuous" and alternative sex styles has enjoyed resurgence in the past few decades.

From of old, however, sex and love were viewed as heavenly gifts, bestowed primarily by the highest of mysteries, the Goddess herself. In a book that has often failed to receive the notice it is due, Merlin Stone probed the parameters of this ancient motif. In her study entitled *When God Was a Woman*, Stone traces the history of humankind's early matrilineal cultures, down to their suppression in the waning millennia just before the Christian era.

From the earliest Neolithic period to the time of the Indo-Aryan invasions (25,000 to 2,400 B.C.), Europe, Greece, and the cultures of the Fertile Crescent worshipped the Queen of Heaven. It was an era when women enjoyed full property rights, could choose from among the males that would father their children, and determine an equitable distribution of the family's wealth. It was the age of the priestess, rather than the priest, a time when many women lived in temple complexes. The women who chose to do so were known as *qadishtu*, "holy women," or were referred to as "sacred temple girls," as Shamhat is called in *The Epic of Gilgamesh*. They were respected devotees of the Heavenly Mother and bestowers of her many gifts--expecially love and sex. Of this phenomenon Stone writes: "Among these people the act of sex was considered to be sacred, so holy and precious that it was enacted within the house of the Creatress of heaven, earth and all life. As one of Her many aspects, the Goddess was revered as the patron deity of sexual love."[47]

From Anatolia to Mesopotamia to Egypt to India, she was known by a variety of names: Aphrodite, Cybele, Inanna, Nammu, Ishtar, Asherah, Ashtarte, Anath, Maat, Isis, Lakshmi, and Kali to name but a few. Numerous plaques, depicting lovers in close embrace, or a woman holding a child, have been excavated at ancient shrine sites. In addition, a trove of texts has survived, in which the role of the Mother Goddess as lover and warrior has been preserved.

Then came the invasions. Wave after wave of migrations. Stone identifies the invaders as descendants of the Maglemosian and Kunda people of the Mesolithic period (15,000 to 8,000 B.C.). They came from the coastal regions and deep forests of north Europe, and from north of the Black Sea, the Caucasus, and Caspian Sea. By 2400 B.C. their presence was felt all along the Neolithic, matrilineal culture line, from Greece to India. Their coming forged a new order, impacting on everything: politics, religion, literature, rights, wealth, the status of women, the soul of what makes a civilization a civilization. The role of the Mother Goddess was subsumed under a panoply of male deities.

---

[47] Merlin Stone, *When God Was a Woman* (New York: Dorset Press, 1976), p. 154.

Yet, for a remaining two and a half millennia her gracious and loving ways would live on, cherished by her conquered worshipers.

In Stone's view, the brutal manner in which she was excoriated in the land of Canaan can still be read in the Old Testament. There the Israelites were commanded to destroy every vestige of her presence. The new, zealous, male-dominated religion of Yahweh could allow no quarter for its older, serene, and sacred sister. She was put to the sword, her "holy women" denounced as whores, her high places and green trees felled by the axe, and sacred images trampled into the dust. Whole villages and cities, children and livestock, were consigned to flames, the *herem*, "the holy ban," as the Hebrew puts it. It is of interest also to note that the Hebrew word for "holy" is *qadosh*, but *qadosh* is now a property of the male God Yahweh. As late as 609 B.C., one of the greatest of Israel's prophets was still railing against the Goddess.

> The children gather wood, the fathers kindle fire, and the women knead dough, to make cakes for the *queen of heaven*; and they pour out drink offerings to other gods, to provoke me to anger.... says Yahweh (Jeremiah 7:18; italics for emphasis).

We can lament history's misappropiation of its past and turn self-righteously from its great reformers, but that will do little good. Instead, one might ask what a more positive interpretation of this past has to offer today. Such has been the approach of many feminist scholars. Carol Christ in particular has rediscovered many valuable nuances that the Goddess concept can signify for women.

In her anthology, *WomanSpirit Rising*, she provides no fewer than four reasons why Goddess symbolism is significant. First, the phenomenon affirms female power by its acknowledgment of the feminine experience as a "beneficent and independent power."[48] To that extent, it liberates women from dependence on male figures and male gods of salvation and it encourages them to trust in themselves. Second, Goddess-symbolism affirms the value of the female body, in all of its cycles of menstruation, birth, and care for the dying. It enables women to realize afresh that their bodies are "the direct incarnation of

---

[48] Carol P. Christ and Judith Plaskow, *WomanSpirit Rising: A Feminist Reader in Religion* (San Francisco: HarperSanFrancisco, 1992), p. 277.

waxing and waning . . . cycles of the universe."[49]   Third, Goddess-symbolism underscores the positive value of the feminine will.   Every woman has as much right to self-determination as any man.   Finally, Goddess-symbolism celebrates a woman's bonds with her sister women, especially the bonding between mother and daughter.   It allows for the rediscovery of newfound beauty and power that are unique to the female gender.

It is doubtful that we will ever again build temples to the Goddess, although some Protestants may consider every cathedral dedicated to the Virgin Mary the equivalent.   Nonetheless, the gifts of sex and love, which the universe and evolution have bequeathed to us, are integral to our wholeness.   They both inform and form the soul of our spirituality, our depth and wonder, our mystery as human beings. If not the greatest gifts, they are at least among the most gracious gifts that keep us human.

---

[49] Ibid., p. 281.

Chapter 13

Life as a Journey

Long before Jason and his Argonauts sailed the Aegean, humanity was on the move: migrating, traveling, in transit. This migrating, traveling, and, later, adventure motif has defined our beingness as much as anything that contributes to our wholeness. It is a facet of the flowing quality of life. It too is of the earth. As a Zen poem captures it:

> When I pass over the bridge
> Lo, the water floweth not, but the bridge doth flow.

The ancient Israelite put it in a creed: "A wandering Aramean was my father" (Deut. 26:5).

We do not know precisely when the first hominids abandoned their African savanna for the long trek north and east. *Ramapithecus* (an early apelike hominid) may well have done so as early as five million years ago. Four million years later, he would be followed by *Homo erectus*, whose line prehistorians hypothesize gave rise to Neanderthal, Cro-Magnon Man, *Homo sapiens*, and finally *Homo sapiens sapiens*, or our own species. By the last Ice Age, the latter were settled in Europe and had spread across Asia, the Pacific, the Bering Strait, and down into the Americas. Their genes, chromosomes, and genetic code still "bleep" in our cells, still inform our subconscious memory, and lie behind our intuitive instincts of awe, fear, wonder, flight.

For centuries, they were food-sharers, food-gatherers, wanderers of steppes, valleys, tundra, plains. Necessity, shifting food habitats, weather cycles, topography kept them on the move. Their lives oscillated between hunger and plenty, fear and respite, sorrow and fitful moments of tenderness.

They buried their dead with their weapons beside them, their knives, beads, and even pouches of grain and seed, as if anticipating a further journey. They left behind their pastel hand-prints and bisons, smudged in smoke and poked on damp cave ceilings, for us to see. Red, yellow, black or white, we are descended from these Pleistocene, ice-age, and stone-age wanderers.

In time, they settled down and created civilizations--in China, India, Mesopotamia, Egypt, Greece, North America, Central America, and elsewhere. But their earliest literature recalls the time when they were still a people on the move: foraging, migrating, wandering in search of survival or adventure. We see it in the poetry of the Vedas, the adventures of Enkidu and Gilgamesh, the wanderings of Abraham, Isaac, Ishmael, and Jacob, the travels of Odysseus and Aeneas, and in the legend of the four migrations, sacred to the Hopi people.

What is the meaning of this journey motif in terms of our present existence? What did humanity lose, for all that it gained, when the wanderer sank beside his pack, exchanged his tent for a hut, his dome of stars for a thatched ceiling, his open plains for a town's walls, his vista of the mountains for obelisks and towers?

Why do we still love to travel, to walk beside the sea, to follow a meandering stream, to hike into the hills, to camp out under the star-nations, to gaze into the twinkling dome of night?

In the West, since childhood, we are reared with notions that life has a goal, some upward call, some definite purpose, which we are meant to serve. We are supposed to move from this point to that point, in search and fulfillment of the "point" of life. As Reinhold Niebuhr puts it : "The meaning of life is more than the living of life."[50]

---

[50] See Reinhold Niebuhr's *The Nature and Destiny of Man* (New York: Charles Scribner's Sons, 1949), especially Part I, where he develops the thesis that man is more than the sum total of his vitalities and natural energies. Niebuhr (1892-1971) is especially remembered for his exploration of forms of pride (spiritual and collective) and their impact upon society.

By that Niebuhr means that we are more than the sum total of our naturalistic drives. Our capacity for transcendence has to be addressed, along with the fact that nothing "worth doing can be achieved in a lifetime." For Niebuhr, as creatures of spirit and nature, only the transcendent God of the universe can speak to our condition.

But what if Niebuhr is wrong? Or at least partly wrong? What if the only "meaning" of life is to live life now, in all of its wonder, adversity, sorrow and joy, and be grateful for the journey? And grateful to the Giver, whether that Giver is nature or God? In the final analysis, no theology of slogans has ever been a true barometer of genuine faith in the Eternal, nor an adequate measure of one's commitment to the value of all living things.

Streams, flowing freely where nature bears them, require no teleological meaning, or predetermined goal, to constitute their beauty, wonder or value. To wander beside a stream, to listen to its murmuring flow, to stare down at the pink, green, and gray gravel that lie on its bottom, and to behold the moss covered rocks that flank its banks is to experience an entity of value in itself. The stream isn't going anywhere, other than to the sea, back into Mother Earth. Yet it is a thing of beauty. In yielding itself to its own journey, it provides a habitat for trout, a mirror for summer's flowers, and a crystalline pathway for ice and snow. "All over the earth the faces of living things are all alike."

What is true of streams is also true of trees, flowers, mountains, and lakes, as well as of deer, birds, wolves, and people. Martin Buber's *I and Thou* demonstrated the capacity we have for relating to every being as a being-of-value, or a being of respect, in and of itself.[51] For Buber, the primary word is *relation*, and I-thou relations are possible with life's three inescapable realms: nature, humanity, and the Eternal. It is only when we enter into I-thou relationships with any entity that we do justice to that reality and ourselves as beings of respect. From an environmentalist's perspective, all who love the land and love wilderness endorse the same timbre, the same emphasis.

---

[51] Martin Buber (1878-1965), a Jewish thinker and student of Hasidic Judaism, is best known for his *I and Thou*, but his *Eclipse of God* and *Tales of the Hasidim* are equally worth reading. His influence upon contemporary Christian and Jewish thought has been profound.

When my two sons and I journeyed West to fish the rivers of Montana and Wyoming, we were startled one morning to hear a wolf pack in pursuit of a moose or deer. It occurred near Sylvan Lake, high in the Yellowstone mountains. Dawn was struggling to arrive over the ice-capped ridges. An eagle floated in the cold sky overhead. The lake lay dark and asleep in shadows. Mist drifted over the waters. Bryan had just joined his fly-rod and was guiding line onto the rod when we heard the pack's howls. Heavy and lonely, hungry and mournful, they echoed across the lake. Suddenly they stopped. They had seen our silhouettes through the mist, the motion of a rod, a reflection in the water. The mountains looked down in silence; the distant green shoreline withdrew its sounds. We stood alone and yet at one: with ourselves, with each other, with the lake, and with the mountains. Bryan spotted the trout, waded out into the cold water, and began casting.

Later that week, while fishing in the northeastern corner of the park, my older son, John, and I spotted large, brown, boxlike animals foraging on a mountain slope above the stream. Through our binoculars we were able to pull them into view: a family of grizzlies, browsing in thickets of berries. That evening, as we returned to our camp, it began to snow. The snow was thin and light. Suddenly it stopped, and the sunlight burst through the clouds. All across the dome of the sky, from west to east, hung a series of rainbows. Their pink and indigo and yellow hues illumined the mist about us. It was Bryan's sixteenth birthday. We watched the phenomenon for a full three minutes, before the rainbows paled and night crept in.

Before flying out of Billings to return home, we drove to the Little Big Horn for one last visit. We stopped by the Custer monument, then followed the ridge to the Reno redoubt. We got out of the car and looked down the slope, toward the river below. Here frightened cavalry men and excited Indians had spilled their blood upon the earth. My sons knew the story of their great-grandmother's birth in 1878, "two years after the Custer massacre," as she was fond of saying. Now through her life and her genetic code we were linked to the essence of this holy spot and, through the mystery of its history and hers, it was bone of our bone.

Life is its own reward. Every moment of the journey is filled with possibilities for experiencing the voice of Being, for discovering some immanent, immediate, and penetrating insight, or filled with possibilities for actions that benefit ourselves and others.

From time to time, summer by summer, my brother and I have hiked various portions of the Appalachian Trail. The most memorable of these was a three-day hike across Mt. Rogers and Whitetop Mountain. It was both an exhilarating and exhausting hike, mostly through mist and drizzle, along mountain ledges and summits, and through thickets of rhododendron in full bloom. We hiked twelve miles the first day, fourteen the second, and nineteen the third. Chicadees and titmice serenaded us. Blue and yellow wildflowers were in bloom, and the high meadows were lush with grass.

The first day it rained heavily. It poured down hard, turning the trail into a creek. Our feet were wet the entire time. We began northeast of Pine Mountain and walked southwest, first across Pine Mountain, then around Mt. Rogers and Whitetop. We saw deer, grouse, turkeys, and wild ponies. The black berries were still green.

We rarely passed anyone. The hikers we met where on their way north, toward Maine. Since it was mid-July, Jack surmised that none of them would make it that year to Maine.

We talked a great deal the first day but hardly said anything the third. It was all I could do to complete the nineteen-mile trek from the base of Whitetop into Damascus.

At one point, for about four miles, we trekked along the ridge of a mountain. The trail followed a rocky incline, flanked by oaks, hickories, and white pine. Moss and mushrooms grew in abundance. Shades of green encompassed us. And always and everywhere loomed the weathered rock. And because of all the rain, rivulets of runoff, streaming into rushing creeks, rumbled past us, often hidden in the rhododendron thickets. But we could hear the creeks, thundering lightly, where they spilled into rivers and larger streams. Except for the waterfalls and birds' songs, the forest was damp and silent, and we passed through cathedral after cathedral of poplars, aglow in trellises of light.

"The hour is coming," said Jesus, "when true worshipers will worship the Father in spirit and truth.... God is spirit, and those who worship him must worship in spirit and truth" (John 4:23). Life's journey is filled with Spirit, however one might wish to define it, and, in truth, it is its own reward. However long, however brief.

"*Einmal und nicht mehr.*" "Once and never again," wrote Rilke. We, who are "the most fleeting of all," live this once *und nicht mehr*. But this once, this having been just once, "even if only once: to have been at one with the earth, seems beyond undoing."[52]

---

[52] See Rainer Maria Rilke's *Duino Elegies*, trans. by Stephen Spender (New York: W.W. Norton, 1967), the Ninth Elegy.

Part II. Transcendence and the Mystery of Human Existence

An Autobiography of the Homeward Journey

Chapter 14

The Descent of Man

Modern science[53] traces human origins to a minimum of 1-2 million years ago, if not at least to 3-4 million years ago. So late a date, however, belies the tantalyzing story of our true beginnings. Humanity is descended (literally) from a line of *hominids* (having to do with mankind) whose ancestors in turn are traceable to *hominoids* (small, arboreal creatures) who lived in treetops some 30 million years ago.

It was somewhere in the dim reaches of this period, placed between the Oligocene and Miocene Epics, that hominoids branched into two main divisions. One would lead to the *pongids*, or apes, the other to the *hominids*, or the family of humankind.

By the mid Miocene Epic (26 million years ago), the first hominoids had already developed upright postures, hand-over-hand travel, a lengthening of limbs, versatile arm and hip sockets, broad chests, and strong collar bones. They had become true "tree-walkers," blessed with an aerobatic agility to explore their endless arboreal domain.

Their canopied environment provided additional incentive toward development, for its vast realm of foliage and flowers, light and sky, supplied not only their shelter and food, but evoked curiosity as well. Brain size increased; sensory powers were quickened. The capacity to feel, touch, and see the world around them also enhanced their self-awareness. Their ability to move about the teeming

---

[53] The data sited in this chapter is drawn largely from Paul Weisz, *The Science of Zoology* (New York: McGraw-Hill Book Company, 1966).

population of the canopy encouraged new patterns of communication, voice variation, social contact. Under such conditions, intelligence increased.

Treelife also contributed to a more secure living environment. Other than falling (a fear we still possess), the snake posed the most significant remaining danger (a life form we abhor as much as they). As larger bodies and thumbs evolved, faster escapes became possible, as well as the snatching up of the new born out of harm's way.

The pongid line remained in the trees, their bodies increased in size, their feet remained handlike. Hominids, however, abandoned their canopy, but just when that occurred is still debatable. Nonetheless, the safety gained in those long years of evolving in that arboreal habitat preserved and made possible the emergence of human beings.

Scientists speculate that the cooler climates of the Tertiary Period (75-11 million years ago), triggered man's "descent." As the atmosphere cooled, forests began to thin. Breaks were created between the earlier continuous stretches of green canopy. Some hominids were forced to descend. Their new ground habitat posed frightening dangers, for members of the cat family and other predators prowled the grasses. Quick getaways became essential. Consequently, new muscles developed, agile feet, stronger thighs and calves. It was during this period (of about 12 million years ago), that "man's most distant" ancestor, in Richard E. Leaky's[54] view, appeared. For Leaky, *Ramapithecus* (a small, apelike creature) provides our best picture of that "gradual transition from ape to hominid." Ramapithecus was a "seed-eater," without canine teeth. He might have used tools, but as Leaky acknowledges, the evidence is lean. Nonetheless, with him began the need of savanna-roaming hominids to form social groups, a key factor in prehistoric man's evolution. For Leaky, the young offspring's dependence on adults for food and protection played a critical role in human development.

With Leaky's exception, most primatologists and anthropologists date mankind's arrival with the fashioning of tools. Prehuman hominids were already using sticks and stones to enhance food gathering and survival. Many biologists, however, link the presence of "man" only with the latter's deliberately fashioning of tools

---

[54] Richard E. Leaky and Roger Lewin, *Origins* (New York: E.P. Dutton, 1979), p. 14.

and other articles, however crude. The arrival at this stage indicates human presence. On the basis of this distinction, both *Australopithecus* of East Africa and *Homo habilis* (whom Leaky dates to 3 million years ago), qualify as early "men," as both made tools and possibly knew "speech."

By the Pleistocene Epoch (1 million years ago), the line that gave rise to modern man flickers more clearly into view. Out of that epoch emerges *Homo erectus*, a true, bipedal, prehistoric man. He made tools, used fire, and cooked food. As a result, his jaw-bone receded and his facial features became more humanlike. Well might he have uttered "speech," rather than grunt or whimper. A food-gatherer, he was still vulnerable to tooth and claw, but his brain volume was only one-third less than ours. We can only imagine the quality of his existence, his flight from danger, his grief when his mate or offspring was mawled. If not his genes, his spirit is in us, and ours in him. Leaky bestows high regard on him, because through *Homo erectus's* many years of evolution, he learned to transport food, water, fire, and above all "experience," the latter requiring language. Leaky also notes the significance of "fire" and the coming of the "hearth." He endows each with mystical powers in their role as shapers of human existence and thought.

The best known prehistoric men, however, were the Neanderthals. They flourished between 150,000 to 25,000 years ago. Their Golden Age coincides with the last Ice Age. At one time it was thought that we were genetically kin to them; however, recent DNA tests indicate otherwise. Neanderthal's realm stretched across Europe. He fashioned many tools, axes, clubs, and household equipment. He left behind neither pottery nor art works. He remained a nomad to the eve of his extinction. Yet, it is with him that scholars of religion beleive "religion" originated.

In their widely accepted book, *A History of the World's Religions* (9th ed.), David and John Noss hypothesize that Neanderthal man's graves more than provide evidence of the dawn of religion. All the necessities for a life after death accompany the dead: food, flints, axes, scrapers. Even their upright position suggests the anticipation of a new day. Neanderthal man also revered bear skulls, placing them in central places, niches, and on elavated slabs, implying their participation in a cult, or a rite of intensification, designed to enhance affinity with the bear.

Scientists theorize that it was *Cro-Magnon Man* (50,000 to 20,000 years ago), however, who actually preceded modern man. He was a true *Homo sapiens.* Though still a member of the Stone Age culture, Cro-Magnon man created bone needles with which he fashioned garments of hides. He was a cave-dwelling hunter, one step up from a food-gatherer, but had yet to domesticate livestock or begin the practice of agriculture. Nonetheless, he achieved a notable capacity for creating works of art and left behind an array of cave murals.

In a manner similar to the Neanderthals, Cro-Magnons buried their dead near grottos and painted their bodies and bones red. They also placed prized ornaments of shell and hair circlets beside them, along with weapons and food. In addition to their stunning murals, the Cro-Magnons created carved bone figures, with distended forms, suggesting pregnancy or their acknowledgment of the phenomenon of fertility. As the Noss writers explain, here was a practice of "a religioaesthetic impulse," celebrating kinship with both animal and human spirits. The office of the shaman seems also to have begun with them, as, in one of their paintings, a bearded figure appears arrayed in antlers, stag ears, bear paws, and a horse's tail. All the touches of ritual, ceremony, animism, and magic accompany the scene.

Somewhere in the late Pleistocene Epoch (20,000 B.C.), our own modern species of *Home sapiens sapiens* emerged. By then, the other species had faded away. He alone stands as the sole survivor of that long hominid line that first experienced self-awareness in the arboreal canopy of the Miocene Epoch and finally made it into the Middle Stone Age of 15,000 to 5,000 B.C. as a human being. There is both beauty and sadness, glory and loss in his story that our very being conceals in our molecular structure as offspring of Gaia.

Now historic man would arrive, along with agriculture, writing, art, houses, complex soical orders, and the phenomenon of religion. And this man, with infinity in his heart, if Tillich is correct, is the being whose soul strains past the planets and the stars to search the twinkling infinity of the heavens for God. With him religion, goddesses, gods, prayers, and angelic beings burst upon the spiritual scene. And we, his modern progeny, are still heirs of his luxuriant thought, imagination, fantasies, spirituality, and fears.

Science offers its own valid assessment of the phenomenon. As the zoologist Weisz notes: "Man certainly is an animal, but an animal with many unique attributes."[55]   It is his brain, however, that makes him genuinely unique and accounts for his marvelous capacities. Weisz continues: "The greatest growth [of the human brain] has occurred in the temporal lobes, which participate in the control of speech, and especially in the frontal lobes, which control abstract thought." But the greatest difference between the hominid man and his pongid cousins lies in his unique ability "to think in a new time dimension,... the future." Thus man "is able to plan, to reason out the consequences of future actions,... to choose by deliberation, and to have aims and purposes, ... to think in symbolic terms,... to envision beauty and to weep and to laugh."[56]

It is the arrival of this species, with its capacity to entertain such "aims and purposes," that constitutes *Homo religiosus*, that one creature whose searching drive constantly puts its existence to the question, as it marvels at the wonder of the universe.   We are that species, the conscious extension of 3.6 billion years of evolving ecosystems, interrelated to and interacting with a biosphere that is both encoded in our genes, as well as bone of our bone and flesh of our flesh. Is it any wonder that we feel a sense of oneness with nature, or carry in our subconscious memory an affinity with its flora and fauna, that whispers to us from every treetop?

---

[55] Ibid., p. 428.
[56] Ibid., pp. 429-30.

Chapter 15

From the Shade of the Forest to Ivy Halls

In the summer of 1953 my father retired from the army, and our family returned south, to Roanoke, Virginia. Aunt Evelyn was still alive, so Roanoke, a three-hour drive from Abingdon, was as close as Dad cared to move.

That fall, I entered North Carolina State College, at Raleigh, as a freshman in the School of Forestry. I had resolved to major in forest mangement, or some branch of forestry, with an eye to working for the U.S. Forest Service upon graduation. The two years I spent at State were filled with courses in soil agronomy, dendrology, botany, zoology, surveying, and the mastering of the, now-defunct, slide rule. Weekends were spent in the field, at a nearby logging camp. It was east of Raleigh in the heart of a vast tract of forest, devoted to raising and experimenting with loblolly pine.

My favorite course was dendrology, in which we learned to identify trees and various select cuts of lumber. Our professor, a Dr. Slocom, would give us a small wedge of wood, which we had to examine and correctly identify as ash, oak, pine, or whatever. We had to be exact, for there are no in-betweens. We used a pocket-sized magnifying glass for examining the wood, so we could count its rings, see its color with greater intensity, and, after shaving a sliver off with a knife, smell it and taste it to determine its genus and species.

One of our textbooks was R. J. Preston's *North American Trees*. Dr. Preston was the dean of the School of Forestry, and his book was highly regarded. To this day, I rarely go into the woods without it, for it is a superb manual for identifying trees. Preston was

a quiet man, with dark, penetrating eyes. He was the first true scholar I
ever met and studied under, the first scholar who possessed a sense of
man's transcendence but a love for the biotic community. I can still
see him, seated at his desk, a professional man of the forest, and a
scientist in the classroom as well as in the field.

That first summer, I worked for the U.S. Forest Service and
was assigned to the Toe-Cane River District of North Carolina. That is
a portion of U.S. Forest lands that extends from Roan Mountain in
Tennessee to Mt. Mitchell, northeast of Asheville, North Carolina.
The Toe-Cane district contains some of the South's highest peaks. We
reran old survey lines, cleared brush along the government's borders,
and rebuilt an occasonal firelane.

I lived in a cabin at the end of a dirt road at the foot of Mt.
Mitchell. The cabin was located in a white pine woods, surrounded by
rhododendron, birch trees, and ferns. My first night, a bear's growl
awoke me around one a.m. The animal suddenly slammed its paws
against the cabin, jarring the windows in the room where I slept. My
only weapon was a macheté, which I kept under the bed, and a .22
pistol, which I had left in the kitchen. I crept out of the sheets and
crouched in the room's corner, the macheté in hand. The bear slammed
its body against the building a second time, then it emitted a loud,
mournful cry and lumbered off in the dark. It never returned. Once I
grew accustomed to the cabin and the pines, I missed the bear and hoped
it would come back. I would search for its paw prints, but of course
never found any. Deer were abundant and drank from the cabin's spring
every morning. I would see them at first light, while I was preparing
oatmeal.

The men with whom I worked were genuine mountaineers.
They wore ankle-high brogans, bib-overalls, and felt hats. They rolled
their own cigarettes and chewed tobacco and were proud employees of
the U.S. Forest Service. They teased me without mercy, did their best
to outwalk me, and taught me numerous things about trees and
mountains, laurel and streams. Each carried a personal talisman and
insisted that I carry one, too. I pretended to be indifferent until an old
fellow by the name of Reedy expressed anxiety about my bringing bad
luck on all of them, "since you'ens ain't got no respect for the wilds."
He gave me a buckeye acorn, which he personally selected and polished.
It was not until years later that I realized how important their talismans
were. Far from being tags of superstition, or animistic ornaments,

their buckeyes, rabbit foots, polished stones, and favorite knifes represented their links with the mystery of being and their relatedness to all "fellow" entities in "the wilds." Their holy talismans protected them and united them with "all their relatives." However primitive the legacy might be, it was contemporary with them.

Somewhere in his bestseller of the 1930s, *Modern Man in Search of a Soul*, Carl Jung tells the story of the African tribesmen who stop suddenly beside a stream. An unexpected "omen" lies across their path. They glance nervously toward each other, then withdraw from the jungle. Jung justifies their action on the ground that each hunter's hidden self had been alerted, and it was wiser to return to the village and there await more propitious signs. In a similar manner, Chief Plenty-Coups of the Crows tells how, time and again, each warrior's talisman, or "medicine bag," saved him in time of trouble, illness, or battle. In the old chief's case, the feathers of a chickadee constituted his fetish. Hung from a hairlock and tucked behind his left ear, the feathers gave him a sense of being inconscipuous, slight, swift, and invisible in battle. For the Crows, the chickadee also represented a willingness to listen, to learn, and to be willing to develop one's mind. All told, each man's "medicine" contributed to his sense of well-being and thus undergirded the well-being of the entire party.[57] So it was for our tiny band of foresters that summer, even if our talismans were relics of the rites of intensification.

Often our work was dangerous, along narrow paths and steep cliffs, and sometimes took us through dry woods, by old mica mines, and across swift streams and rocky rivers. Not once, however, did our work team experience an accident, a snakebite, or an injury. We were in tune with our biotic community, its fauna and flora, its rocks and waterfalls, its forests and thickets of laurel and rhododendron. And we each carried a talisman, our personal form of "medicine."

The closest we came to danger occurred high in the mountains, near the Tennessee border. We were working in a meadow, at an altitude of about four thousand feet. We were running a government boundary line when we came upon a farmer mowing hay. His mowing machine was of the horsedrawn vintage. He had pulled it under the shade of locust trees to rest his horse and was trying to roll a cigarette.

---

[57] Frank B. Linderman, *Plenty-Coups: Chief of the Crows* (Lincoln: University of Nebraska Press, 1962).

His hands were trembling, and the shredded tabacco had tumbled everywhere. Reedy tried to get him to speak, but the man could only grunt and point toward a rail fence. We walked over to discover five rattlesnakes, torn open by the mowing machine, their bodies neatly stretched out over one of the rails. "There's more o'em out there," the farmer said, "but I ain't goin' back." For the next two hours we worked the meadow, setting up our compass line with nervous caution, and sweeping the tall grass, back and forth, with our heavy bush-hook blades.

One weekend, toward the end of summer, I decided to explore an abandoned mica mine near the cabin. I had to cross several streams to reach it, then thread my way through a bottom of tall ferns. I had strapped a shiny, new leather holster, with my .22-caliber pistol in it, on my right side. Instead of wearing boots that day, I had slipped into a pair of moccasins. In my jean pockets I carried the cabin keys, a knife, and my buckeye acorn. After crossing the last stream, I spotted the mine's entrance and piles of shiny mica shards. Mica is like opaque mother-of-pearl: smoky, lustrous, pale blue and at times even silver. I could hardly wait to pocket a handsome shard. Out of the corner of my eye, I noticed a particularly bright orange and metalic looking pile. I stepped toward it and bent down. It was a coiled rattlesnake! It had not moved or quivered. Its tongue worked the air. Instinctively, I leaped back a good five feet. With pulsating temples, I drew the .22, aimed it nervously at the coiled heap, and emptied the revolver. I only hit the snake once, but in the head. As it died, its body slowly uncurled. Its white underside rolled up and blood trickled out behind an eye. Its beauty was gone. And so was its life. The thought of cutting off its rattlers filled me with shame. I left it there in the shade of the ferns, under the hemlock canopy overhead. I rewaded all the streams, as if to atone for its death, but no solace was forthcoming.

Contact with danger, however, constituted but a small facet of the summer's work. Every day brought forth some new aesthetic wonder to be experienced. They came in many forms. Frequently we flushed grouse, passed flocks of wild turkeys, or paused to observe a doe and her speckled fawn. In the high mountains we spotted many indigo buntings, scarlet tanagers, warblers, and, of course, towhees. Throughout most of June, and even into July, mountain laurel and rhododendron were still in bloom, and their soft, pink and white lacy blossoms littered the mountain paths. Once, one of the younger men climbed a basswood tree and brought down fresh hunks of sourwood honey. He kept the bees away by smoking a pipe and fanning the hive with his hat.

My father came to stay with me that last week of August. He loved the oak woods, the stands of white pine, the birches, fern and poplar.

"You mustn't tell your mother about this place," he said. "She would die if she realized how isolated you've been."

I agreed, but had never felt alone, at least not after the first week. I told my father about the bear, but I kept the killing of the rattlesnake to myself.

When I returned that fall, I began attending a Westminster Fellowship group at the West Raleigh Presbyterian Church. That is where the cutest girls hung out. Little did I know how that innocent quest for girls would change my life. John Fire Lame Deer loves to write about how he used to "count coup on the girls" when he was young. But just to kiss and hold hands was a coup for me--at least in the fifties. But the "coup" was on me. The group's director was a young seminary graduate, whose commitment to people and ideals was positive and compelling. My enthusiasm for forestry slowly began to wane, as I read, for the first time, the gospels. I had never read them before. And I wanted to be like that Galilean of the morning sky, who also arose before dawn, and went into the hills to pray to his Heavenly Father. I did not know where the quest would take me, but I knew I had to follow it. I was baptized and turned my face away from the forest and matriculated the following fall at Davidson College, to study philosophy, history, and literature. I entered the world of ivy walls, and I loved every minute of it.

Socrates, Plato, Euripides, Plutarch, Emerson, Whitman, Wordsworth, Kierkegaard, Tolstoy, Dostoyevsky. Hemingway, Faulkner, Steinbeck, Luther, Barth, Nietzsche, Tillich. I wandered into a world from which I never wanted to withdraw. By the time of my graduation, my soul had set five goals for itself: become a minister, travel like Hemingway, become a professor, write scholarly articles, and leave behind at least one book worth reading, something that would survive Hemingway's famous "built-in, shock-proof, shit detector." Or at least something Granny herself might have enjoyed reading.

In the fall of 1958 I entered Union Theological Seminary in Richmond, Virginia, in pursuit of my first goal. But a year and a half later, I was floundering in doubts, in simple existential despair. I was too much a child of Socrates, of Hemingway, of North Carolina State, and of Nietzsche to swill just anything offered under the rubric of dogma. My spirit was dying, and I was lost as to what to do. But I was open to change, open to anything that might happen, when Balmer Kelly invited me to drop by his office.

Kelly was our New Testament professor. He had worked his own way through the quest of the historical Jesus problem and was, just then, moving toward Bultmann's[58] existentialist position. Bultmann held that we can never know who the historical Jesus is; nonetheless, Jesus can serve in a redemptive capacity, enabling us to overcome our ambiguities and sense of alienation, finding new meaning in him. So Kelly took me aside. He understood why I hurt, and he let me tell him the truth.

"I need to leave here. I'm sinking under the farce of all this dogma, of all the falsehood heaped against Jesus. I can't believe that he is anything other than a man. I need to breathe again, find myself again. Maybe even find God."

Kelly smiled. "Ben, I've just returned from France. There's a center there for spiritual retreat, a kind of Protestant monastery, under the direction of a most extraordinary man, an André de Robert. They're game to take on an American for a year, he said, if you'd care to go."

"I don't have any way to get there. I can't ask my parents to fund such a trip."

"I can help you with the travel, one way, if you'll let me."

Hey hey! Great-grandfather! I sat there, not knowing what to think. My body began to tremble, my shoulders sagged. "Yes, I'll go."

---

[58] Rudolf Bultmann (1884-1976) was a New Testament professor at the University of Marburg, Germany. He is best known for his program of "demythologization." Bultmann argued that Jesus' era endorsed a three-story mythological view of the universe: heaven "above," hell "below," and the earth caught in between. For Bultmann, the real Jesus of history was a captive of that outlook and cannot be appreciated save in its terms. Yet, for a modern era, the essence of Jesus' insight can be captured by interpreting his worldview from an existentialist perspective, in which Jesus helps us overcome our own anxieties and ambiguities by radically trusting in the goodness of God, just as the historical Jesus did.

Thus, that February 1960, I set sail aboard the *Queen Mary* for a year of monastic life in France.

Chapter 16

Villemétrie

Le Centre de Villemétrie, as the community was called, was located just east of Senlis, an hour's drive north of Paris. Senlis was an ancient town, dating back to the early Middle Ages, with cobble-stoned streets and a small cathedral. Joan of Arc had passed through Senlis and, earlier, Charlemagne. Concrete pillboxes from World War II guarded the narrow roads, leading into the town. A cemetery, with rows of weathered stone crosses, all dating from the Great War, looked out over green hedges and fields of black farm soil. I visited it once, and was shocked to discover that an entire company of North African Legionnaries was buried there.

I arrived in the winter when it was very cold. One of the brothers met me at the bus station. I spoke no French; he spoke no English. He put my bags in the back of his *deux-chevaux*, smiled, and off we drove for Villemétrie.

Kelly had tried to prepare me.

"Ben, there's as much truth attached to de Robert as legend, but let me tell you what I know. Sometime, early after the war, de Robert completed his seminary training and received a call to a church in *le Midi*, or the southern part of France. He was a bachelor and thus was able to devote himself to his preaching and tiny parish. The story is that he was preaching on the text: 'sell all that you have, give it to the poor, and come follow me,' when, after the sermon, a stranger, who had attended the service, said to him, 'Pastor, if you believe that, why don't you do it?'

"All that night de Robert pondered the stranger's words. He hardly slept. Then early the next morning, he gathered what possessions he had, gave most of them to the poor, save for a watch repair kit and a few personal belongings, mounted his bike, and rode off into the countryside. He had no idea where he was to go, or what he was to do.

"As he rode along, toward noontime, he saw a group of farmers, stopped for their repast in the field. The region was predominantly Catholic, and the bishop of the diocese had imposed a ban on the area's flock, which meant they couldn't receive communion or take mass, until they accepted whatever it was the archbishop wanted them to do.

"De Robert stopped and walked out to where they were eating, sat down among them, and began to share their meal. Midway through, he lifted a piece of bread. '*Ceci est mon corps*,.... this is my body, broken for you,' he said. Then he broke it, and passed it along to the others. Then he held up a cup of wine: 'This is the cup of the new covenant, shed for the remission of sins. All of you, drink of it.' And he passed it around to the men.

"After that, villagers awaited his arrival wherever he went, invited him into their homes, listened as he read from the gospels, and received communion after meals. In time, the Reformed Church of France came to André and asked him to settle on an estate, to provide spiritual respite for hungry souls. They promised he could have a small *équipe*, a contingent of brothers, to help him, and that they would fund it as long as people came."

Kelly smiled. "You'll like de Robert. But it won't be easy. You can still change your mind."

Villemétrie was situated on the slope of a hill on an old estate. The main chateau was a four-story stuccoed house, with a steep thatched roof, and grand French windows that opened onto a courtyard of fine gravel and trimmed hedges. *La grande maison*, as the chateau was called, was used only on the weekends, when retreats were held. The *équipe* lived in the *petite maison*, which had been the servants' quarters under the previous owners.

The brothers were waiting for us when the driver and I arrived. They were wearing blue smocks. I could see a tie or two here and there. And some of them wore sandals, as cold as it was. I was taken to

André and introduced. A black-bearded Alsacian by the name of Gaston served as our interpreter. "I am from the same country as Schweitzer," he beamed.

André rose from his desk. He was a stocky man, about five-feet-ten, with a wide forehead, and a cleft chin. His eyes were oval and dark gray, and his cheekbones were high and large. He, too, wore a blue smock. His hair was gray. He pushed his glasses back over his forehead. *"Ah, bon!"* he said. *"Notre nouveau frère."* His smile disarmed any apprehension I felt.

It would be months before I could carry on a fluent conversation with André, for he spoke no English, though he could read it. After Gaston left the community, I became de Robert's interpreter, whenever American or English visitors dropped by.

My first task was to learn French, Gaston being the teacher. After a novice's month, I took the three vows: poverty, chastity, and obedience. I knelt in the chapel, which was a room on the third floor of *la grande maison*, and pledged to cooperate with André and the brothers, share their life of simplicity and study, and fulfill whatever tasks the community assigned. Since I held a bonafide American driver's license, I was appointed the community's official chauffeur and general supply and handyman as needed. My assignment was quite a boon, because it freed me from many mundane chores at the Center and provided for excursions far and wide from Villemétrie, which often took me into Paris.

I wanted so much to talk to André those first months. But the language barrier was too severe. André was just then into Barth,[59] as Karl Barth's works were being translated into French at that time. Through Gaston, I tried to introduce him to Tillich, but André was fascinated with Barth's "strange new world of the Bible." For Barth, the Bible contains more than just the history of the Israelites and their understanding of God. It is the supreme place where God meets

---

[59] Karl Barth (1886-1968), Swiss-born theologian, considered by many to be the greatest theologian of the twentieth century. He challenged the liberal Christian view of his day, which spoke glibly of the Fatherhood of God and the brotherhood of man, insisting instead that the Bible is more than a record of Israelite religion and early Christian mythology. Rather, the Bible is the instrument by means of which God, in all God's mystery, speaks to the souls of anxious seekers.

humanity, in spite of humankind's finitude. For Barth, the finite can never grasp the Infinite. Only the Infinite can bridge the gap and reveal itself to mankind. In Barth's mind, Eternity enters time in the story of the Bible, thus what we discover there is not dogma about God, but God, in all God's selfhood. André found Barth's analysis comforting, if not bold, and much to his liking.

My own palaver about finitude, anxiety, nonbeing, and the threat of meaninglessness only brought smiles to de Robert. He was beyond anxiety, because he had already yielded his heart to the Eternal Now, to the Infinite within. But at the time, I could not see that. Besides, deep within, I wanted so much to believe that God existed, that Christ was his true Son, that we lived in a world where "angels bending low to earth ... touch their harps of gold." I wanted the myth of Jesus's birth, his miracles, and his resurrection to be factual, actual events of history, though in my heart I knew that all this had to be *Vorstellungen* and nothing more. Moreover, the idea of *Vorstellungen* was still abstract and the magnitude of its power had not yet sunk into my soul.

As problematic as it was, it was easy to talk about Tillich's "courage to be," but it was quite another thing to seize existence, as André had, and to live it with simple courage.

Kelly was right, however, in sending me to Villemétrie. For the community soon began to exercise its healing powers. After the evening meal, and an hour or two for socializing, music, and reading, André assembled us by the fireplace, with Bibles in hand. We would read the lectionary's prescribed selections for the next day, then select a memory verse, or *capitule* in French, which we would hide in our hearts to reflect on the following day. Once we had agreed upon the passage, we were dismissed to our room and to the office of silence, until after the morning chapel and breakfast. Toward the end of the *petit déjeuner*, André would look up from his *café-au-lait* and say, "The Lord be with you," and we would respond, "and with thy spirit."

I still have my French Bible and all of the *capitules* underlined that we used that year. Their cathartic power still embraces me, some three decades later. For example, from Paul's Thessalonian correspondence: "Create a spiritual house," "Do not render evil for evil, but on the contrary, bless," "Abide in him with a firm faith," "Believe that the Lord's patience exists for your salvation." And from the book of Proverbs: "The fear of the Lord is the beginning of wisdom," "Do not be wise in your own eyes," "Guard your heart more than anything else," "Whoever seeks me will find me," "It is the Lord who weighs the heart."

Not far from *la grande maison* began the forest of Senlis. Hemingway mentions it in *A Moveable Feast* and *The Sun Also Rises*. It was a large forest of pine and ferns and of footpaths and bridlepaths for horseriders. On Sunday afternoons, following a retreat's departure, I would walk those woods. A cavalry unit, attached to the Foreign Legion and stationed near Senlis, would often gallop through the forest, along the trails. I would hear them coming and climb a sandy hill to watch them pass below. I can still see the riders in their khaki uniforms, desert hats, and black boots. The horses, for the most part, were gray.

I would seek out a quiet place, sit under a tall pine, and stare out across the forest. I had come so far. Still, I was at home. The forest was ever about me, with its ferns and soft pine needles. I had abandoned the forest for "God," yet "God" had not taken the forest from me. After luxuriating in the silence and beauty of the woods, I would take out my pocket New Testament and read from the Psalms in the back. "If I ascend to heaven, thou art there. If I make my bed in Sheol, behold, thou art there.... even the darkness is not dark to thee." Sometimes I would sit there and stare off at the forest. I wanted to embrace true existence, without having to define it to death, but did not know how. Yet I was ever in its presence, never far from its heartbeat. For its heartbeat was in me. Still, I would come away consoled. On the one hand sad, yet on the other whole, like Jacob, limping arcoss the Jabbok.[60] All the while, I was in the presence of Being, even if I did not know it.

Life in community was far from toilsome, and often filled with levity. Anyone who withdraws from the world into a monastic community is in for a shock, if not for a lot of fun, laughter, and teasing. And the brothers of Villemétrie were masters at all three. As the brothers got to know me, they would imitate my mountaineer lope and the way I cocked my cap back on my forehead. "J-e-a-n Wayne!" they would tease. "Bee-ig J-e-a-n Wayne!"

"*Non!* C'est J-O-H-N!" I would correct them. "J-O-H-N!"

"J-E-A-N!" they would reply. "*Oui?*"

---

[60] See Genesis 32:22-32.

"*Non!* 'J-o-h-n.' *Mais 'J-e-a-n' ça va bien assez.* Close enough. Ok!"

They would smile, because they had got me to say "John" and a few other words in English and they liked my southern accent, my *patois.*

André loved *le cinéma* and would often take us on Tuesday evenings to see a movie. His favorites were fast-action spy movies, with lots of car chases, wrecks, tough guys talking tough talk, and, of course, always the good-looking blonde. "*Voilà le monde*," he would announce, as we drove back. Sometimes we would stop at a café and talk. "*En notre temps, c'est très difficile de precher le royaume de Dieu.*" He would drop his voice, as if searching for the right words. "*On doit ... l'incarné, ... en notre ... pauvreté ... et ... patience, en notre ... espérance ... et ... faits.*" André knew that words alone could not communicate the Kingdom of God. Its reality could only be embodied in one's poverty and patience. One's hope and deeds. But by "poverty," André meant what Socrates had taught his Athenians, and the Buddha his disciples in the principle of "emptiness," that is, not to pretend to know what one does not know, but to be open and humble before the mystery of being. André's favroite text was: "Blessed are the poor in spirit, for theirs is the kingdom of God" (Matt. 5:5).

Most evenings, we sat around the fireplace and listened to music or read from a favorite book. The Center had a rich record-album collection of classical and contemporary music and a library of classics. Everything from Dvorak's *New World Symphony* to Louis Armstrong's jazz was available. I read Stendhal's *Le Rouge et Le Noir* and *Ivanoé* that first winter, along with numerous selections of Kierkegaard and French poetry. There was a poem in particular that I came to love, because it embodied my sense of being at the time. I have forgotten the author's name, but not the poem:

> I go where the winds blow
> Without joy, without sorrow.
> I go where all things go
> Where go the leaf of the rose
> And the leaf of the laurel.

As a child of the laurel, and a child of the rhododendron, I could identify with the suspension of judgment the poet was offering, like my grandmother's silence to the old man's question. The earth speaks for itself, along with the rose and the laurel, along with the pine and the fern. The poem depicted the inner me with immediate directness. Who was I? Where was I going? I felt like Kierkegaard's[61] "aesthetic man," lost at the "aesthetic stage of life," an observer, a traveler, without joy, without sorrow.

André also enjoyed hiking and would organize "outings" that took us to the parks about Versailles and *la grande forêt de Fontainebleau*. The latter was a magnificent woods of oak and pine, ferns, gray outcroppings, and sandy paths. Save for the sand, I felt I was back somewhere high in the Appalachians, at home in the Knobs.

That June, André summoned me and one of the brothers to his office.

"We'll be moving soon. Our directors have bought an old estate, southeast of Paris, complete with a chapel and park. Our Senlis days are over. I want you two to go to the new estate and prepare it for our move. You'll leave tomorrow, and we'll join you in about a week."

He handed me several hundred francs. "That will tide you over until we arrive. The nearest town is La Ferté-Alais." He then spread out a map and pointed to a crossroads, to the north of La Ferté-Alais. *"Voilà! Tu le vois?"*

"Oui. I see it."

"Bon." Everything was settled. He folded up the map. There was a soft glint in his eyes. *"Le Seigneur soit avec vous,"* he smiled, as he handed me the map.

The next morning, before we left, he came out to the courtyard where we were standing and kissed me on the neck. He kissed the other brother in the same manner. We were his fellow brothers, *ses frères*, but we were more like his sons. We got in the *deux-chevaux* and drove off. Midway down the drive I stopped the vehicle, rolled down my window, and stared back at *la grande maison*, its thatched roof, stuccoed exterior, and grand windows. Beyond its slope, I could see the first rise

---

[61] Soren Kierkegaard (1813-1855), the father of modern existentialism. Kierkegaard distinguishes between three stages of life: the aesthetic, in which one is primarily a detached observer; the ethical, in which one strives to live by society's codes and customs; and the religious, in which one lives exclusively for God, whatever the emotional and cultural cost.

of *la forêt de Senlis* and its tall pines. A rider, just then, burst into the sunlight for an instance, then disappeared. I rolled the window back up, and we drove on into Senlis and the road to Paris.

Chapter 17

The Eternal Human Condition

The new chateau paled in comparison to the grandeur of the *grande maison* at Senlis. It was a three-story, seventeen-room mansion, with servants' quarters in the loft, with a full basement and recreational hall downstairs, complete with a bar and a tiled floor for dancing. A spacious courtyard graced its entrance from the road. A high stone wall, covered with ivy, and an entrance gate of wrought iron gave it an air of seclusion. Slate steps, with ivy covered metal banisters, led from the courtyard to the mansion's main entrance. Large pots of bright red geraniums bordered the courtyard. To the left of the mansion, was another walled courtyard, more quarters, workshops, and a chapel. The chapel sported a large stained-glass window, which had been dedicated by a bishop under former owners. Walls surrounded the entire estate, and the back of the house, which was actually its front, looked across a lush lawn and up an alleyway of oaks and linden trees that led, in turn, to the park and its many pathways.

I was delighted with our new home--stunned, to tell the truth. My companion Jean and I wasted no time unlocking the gate and setting about our tasks. To our joy, we discovered a wine cellar stocked with racks of dusty bottles of red and white wine. We opened one after the other only to discover that they had turned to vinegar. It took us the entire week to clean up the huge house and prepare for the brothers' arrival. An old gardener, by the name of Pierre, came with the estate, but he kept his distance from our chores. "My job is the garden," he smiled, as he raised a glass of wine that first evening.

The next morning, before sunrise, I walked the paths through the park to discover still another treasure: two statues, one of Apollo and one of Artemis, the god of enlightenment and the goddess of the hunt, the goddess of animals and the woods. For the rest of my stay at the Center, whenever I was not working, I fled to this park. It was no forest of Senlis, but it became my *petit knobs*, where I could commune with wind and sky, earth and trees, with the silent ground of being.

That fall, I found myself growing aloof. I was ready for something more, though I did not know what. In the evenings, I would listen to Dvorak's *New World Symphony*, finding special meaning in the second movement, "Going Home." In it, Dvorak has captured that soulful quality of the South, and it tugged on my heart heavily. I could see Granny, Aunt Evelyn, Uncle Clark. The farm, the hills, the red soil. The steep hill that I had so often climbed. The cedar ridges in the wind. The fields of corn and tobacco. The cattle, sheep, and hogs. The bottoms layered in fog. I could see Captain John, galloping into battle to the sound of musketry, envelopped in clouds of gun powder. I wanted to go home, yet I had not found what I was seeking. What was it? What was I to do?

About that time, André instituted a new office for the community. He had begun reading Bonhoeffer[62] and wanted to make our brotherhood more "spiritual." So he set up times when each of us would visit him to discuss our heart's baggage or longings.

It must have been in mid-November. A light snow had fallen on the ground. It was bleak and very cold. It was my time. My time for the office with André.

"*Mon, cher*, you seem so sad. Where is your 'bee-ig' smile? What has happened to *notre frère*? What is it with thee?" he asked.

"I don't know. *Je ne sais pas exactement.* God seems so far away ...."

He smiled. "*Dieu*? And just what is 'God'? And what is 'away'? Huh?"

---

[62] Dietrich Bonhoeffer (1906-1945), Christian theologian, German pastor, participated in the failed attempt to overthrow Hitler, was excuted on April 9, 1945, just days before the collapse of Nazi Germany. He is best remembered for his *The Cost of Discipleship, Life Together,* and *Letters and Papers from Prison.*

He was seated at his desk. I was seated in a cane-bottomed chair, several feet past his desk.

"*Alors*! What is God?" He looked at me with his gray eyes, and then out into the courtyard. "God? Somewhere along the line, Bultmann offers this definition." He cleared his throat. "God? 'God … is the manifestation … of the mystery … of our human condition.' That is God. And that God is never far away. But in thee, *en toi*." He paused. "Tell me about yourself. Please."

I sat in silence for a while. "I have so many doubts," I began. "I really don't believe in … in anything that you're supposed to. My soul is just filled with doubt, a gnawing emptiness. I don't know what to do."

"*Eh, bien*! Listen. And think with me. Remember what Paul says about faith, that it's a gift. *C'est un cadeau.* Some of us aren't given faith, but are given a different gift."

He looked at me and then out into the courtyard again, where snow was falling afresh. I turned to watch it myself. The flakes were large and coming down rapidly. It was very beautiful, but I could feel my heart beating, as I was wondering what André was going to say.

"*Eh, bien*," he repeated. He leaned forward and smiled. "It is so clear, *mon cher*. Don't you see it? God hasn't left you giftless. God has given you a gift. A very special gift. A special *don*. But it is the gift of doubt. *Le doute! Voilà le don* that God has given you."

He asked me to kneel, and he put his right hand on my head.

"Dear Lord Jesus, bless your dear brother Ben, and fill his heart with your presence … and your joy."

I walked back out into the courtyard and toward my quarters, behind the chapel. I remember turning, to watch my steps "fill up with snow." Standing there in the silence, I felt like a monad, suspended in a world of Leibnizian monads, soft and white. I held my hand out to catch some flakes. It was very cold. I tightened the scarf about my neck and pressed on toward our sleeping quarters. I opened the door, closed it quietly, and then hurried toward my desk. Then I knelt beside it and wept.

Chapter 18

The Rites of Passage

Life is a process, a journey of many transitions, as we migrate from stage to stage. As we have seen, the ancient rites of passage were founded on this wisdom. My year with André provided such a passage for me.

Women understand and embody this wisdom in a more complex way than men. They are closer to the cycles of nature. Men, especially young men, are more abstract. They retain their idealism longer and continue their quest for absolutes long after women have accepted the mystery of their beingness. As we noted earlier, the very body of a woman incarnates the waxing and waning of the cycles of the universe, the ebb and flow of life, in both her menstruation and her childbearing capacity. The regenerative powers of nature lie within her.

John Fire Lame Deer tells of a Native American artist whose paintings of western sky and prairie are stunning. One in particular caught his eye--a pastel, velvety rendering of soft hills, a valley, and spring. His artist friend explained. The two rounded hills symbolized his wife's breasts, the grassy prairie her stomach, and the valley and spring her *winyan shan*, her "holy essence."[63]

Women, by nature, are forced to accept their "holy essence," their linkage with the cycles of life, long before men even wake up to the journeying process. I was twenty-four when André's words severed my metaphysical umbilical cord and set me free from a placenta of dying assumptions. Until then, I had based my questions about God,

---

[63] Lame Deer, p. 109.

meaning, and "absolutes" on the assumption that life's "holy essence" lay outside and not within the mystery of our beingness. But that God should be the manifestation of the mystery of our human condition meant that God was within. God was already a reality within me, seeking to come into consciousness. The infinite mystery of the cosmos, cause of my evolving genetic code, or Tillich's "ground of being," or the Lakota *Wakan Tanka*, the Great Mystery, was already within.

Later, during graduate studies, I discovered Tillich's discussion of the above. Tillich argues that there are primarily only two ways of approaching a philosophy of religion, or of coming at God. One is from without, in which we posit God as something outside ourselves and our universe. Such a God must "break in" from without in this scheme. This was Barth's approach. God is not so much the Infinite within, but the wholly transcendent God who stands outside the universe. God is its creator and transcends it, but God is unlike anything or anyone a finite human mind can grasp. That is why God has to "break" into the world and reveal the true nature of God. Mankind cannot reach God on its own. But such an approach requires an epistemology, a way of knowing God, in which God's existence can be proved, or at least demonstrated as credible, which is very difficult to do. The other approach is from within. Tillich calls it the "ontological approach." By "ontological" he means beingness itself. In Greek, the word *ontos* means "being." Who doubts one's own being, or its mystery, or one's encounter with moments of beauty, goodness, and truth? For Tillich, to know such moments is to know "the ground of being," or the depth of being; it is to sense the very mystery of God. As such God requires no further proofs, but only clarification, which the symbols, or *Vorstellungen*, of the biblical story provide.

That my need to question every facet of the mystery was in my marrow (my "divine gift," as André saw it), meant that I was free to interpret the mystery however my experience warranted it.

I could claim my rural heritage, my love for sky and soil, rivers and trees, and not feel that I was betraying myself, or God. I needed no higher purpose than life itself, the journey, in all its flow and change, excitement and struggle, to justify meaning. Least of all, did I require a dogma to assure me of a life after this one to render the present joyful, rewarding, or of value. Slowly the meaning of the Eternal Now began to make sense.

Not all of this occurred to me in that moment with André, but I left his study in a mood of pensive serenity. A human being, humble and "empty" before the mystery of the universe, became the Christ for me, the Buddha for me, the power behind the winds of the four quarters. He helped me wake up and see that the "emptiness" within myself was the mirror of the "ground of being." I was already staring at the face of God. I was already in the presence of the Buddha essence, the Great Spirit, the Eternal Now. I was already experiencing the manifestation of the mystery of our human condition. God was within, however transcendent, as well.

In a more modern vein, we are part of the mystery of being. It pulsates within us, transcends and indwells us. It asks nothing of us, takes nothing from us, and gives us everything in return. When we acknowledge its givenness as a form of grace, empty ourselves of pretension and craving, and come before the presence of the mystery with reverence, we are the richer, and our journey a treasure.

From a scientific perspective, the elemental forces of the universe are within. We are creations of cosmic dust and glowing debris. The life forces of the universe come into consciousness in us. And to live in harmony with them is not only to know peace, but is the way of ultimate wisdom.

There are two Christian hymns that exemplify this wisdom, each in its own way. They symbolize in a poetic and spiritual form what modern science offers from its objective side. One is abstract, lofty, and philosophical. The other is direct, simple, and personal. Both acknowledge the transcendence and immanence of the *Wakan Tanka*, the Great Mystery. They represent a common ground for expressing the universal experience of humankind.

> Immortal, invisible, God only wise
> In light inaccessible hid from our eyes....
> To all, life Thou givest--to both great and small;
> In all life Thou livest, the true life of all.

> This is my Father's world: He shines in all that's fair;
> In the rustling grass I hear Him pass, He speaks to me everywhere.

The Lakota Plains Indian could have chanted these hymns, as well as the Indo-Aryans who created the Vedas, and the Hindu sages who composed the *Bhagavad-Gita*.

When we stop to reflect on the phenomenon of religion, it finally dawns on one that the Buddha essence, the "ground of being," the *Wakan Tanka*, and the Tao are pictorial ways of acknowledging the same Mystery. Their cultural forms vary, but each has to do with reverence for life. Each calls for an "emptying" of the self in the face of Being. They encourage a form of spirituality toward the mystery of existence. In this they differ from science, which tries to be objective. Yet even scientists are awed by the grandeur of the universe, its age, composition, energy; its past, present, and future; its vulnerability to its own forces.

What cannot be denied is our affinity with nature, with the regenerative and ebbing cycles of the universe, which both underlie and pervade our beingness. They come into consciousness in us. To see ourselves akin with all of this, and each of us akin with one another, and all of us akin with all of nature is the only certainty we have.

To wait upon the coming dawn, to watch the evening sun go down, to listen to the silence deep within, to greet the universe with awe, whether in ourselves, nature, or others, and to care for all entities as if they were a *thou*, that is the heart of "religion."

One night, at a time when I had been immersed in studying Buddhism for several months, the Buddha came to me in a dream. He came in the form of the Dalai Lama, who in Tibetan Buddhism is the incarnation of the compassionate spirit of the Buddha. I recognized him by his smile, his round glasses, his fiery vermilion robe, and gentle eyes. "What do you want?" he asked. I was quite stunned by so frank and unsettling a question. "I want ... truth ... beauty ... goodness," I mumbled. Then the Dalai Lama stretched out his arms, the folds of his robe resplendent with light. "Behold, receive them," he said. "For they are yours."

I awoke, breathless, clammy, hot, the hair on my arms tingling. It had been so real. He is right, I thought. All the truth, goodness, and beauty we could ever want is already here. All we have to do is accept it, receive it, live it.

Chapter 19

The Cycles of Time

"For every thing there is a season, and a time for every matter under heaven," writes Qoheleth, the author of the book of Ecclesiastes. He then goes on to list fourteen doublets of twenty-eight seasons. They too bear witness to the passages of life and to the journey motif:

> a time to be born, and a time to die;
> a time to plant, and a time to pluck up what is planted;
> a time to kill, and a time to heal;
> a time to break down, and a time to build up;
> a time to weep, and a time to laugh;
> a time to mourn, and a time to dance;
> a time to throw away stones, and a time to gather stones together;
> a time to embrace, and a time to refrain from embracing;
> a time to seek, and a time to lose;
> a time to keep, and a time to throw away;
> a time to tear, and a time to sew;
> a time to keep silence, and a time to speak;
> a time to love, and a time to hate;
> a time for war, and a time for peace (Eccl. 3:2-8).

The number twenty-eight is transparent, as there are twenty-eight days in a lunar month. To my knowledge, however, no one has analyzed the number "fourteen." Why fourteen doublets? Reflection offers an intriguing solution.

The ancient Israelites observed a lunar-solar calendar. Under such a method of reckoning, there are twelve lunations in a lunar-solar year. The early Israelite Tribal League was founded on a confederacy of tribal families who needed each other and who, in turn, shared responsibility for guarding the shrine site for a lunar month. Later, Israel's storytellers embodied this social structure in the saga of Jacob and his twelve sons. It was a mythic way of giving a sacred dimension to the twelve tribes and justifying their land-claims at the time. But it was the cycles of the lunar year that underlay their statehood. The number twelve also represented the twelve directions of the earth, the twelve directions of the winds, the hours of the day and the hours of the night at the spring and fall equinoxes. Twelve represented the complete circle, the cycle of the year. Passover came in the spring; the harvest festivals and days of rememberance in the fall. If that accounts for "twelve," how do we arrive at fourteen? *Zenith* and *nadir*, or the sky above and the earth beneath, as in Black Elk's prayer, add the missing two and equal to "fourteen."

When one turns to the Plains Indians of North America, one discovers a similar calendar and way of reckoning seasons. Time is measured by the moons, by the winds of the four quarters, by the symbol of the circle, by the cyclical view of life, and its timeless, flowing quality. They enshrined the latter in their tepees, their hoops, their drums, their dances that moved in clockwise and counter-closkwise patterns. The number "four" was especially sacred, as were the four corners of the earth (remember Alexander's theory). The south represented life, birth, and harvest; yellow was its color. The west represented youth, manhood, vitality; the prime of one's life; black, the color of the storm cloud, was its hue. The north represented maturity, grayness, winter, with its white and snowy cover. The east: sunrise, fire, light, wisdom; its color red. And then, childhood again, as old age turned full harvest and yielded itself back to Mother Earth. The number "four" also stood for the virtues that males were encouraged to possess: bravery, generosity, endurance, and wisdom; and for women: bravery, generosity, truthfulness and child-bearing.[64] For every turn there was a season, a time for every matter under heaven.

Joseph Bruchac, a descendant of Abenaki people, explains that among many North American Indians, a lunar year of thirteen "moons"

---

[64] Ibid. See Lame Deer's discussion of the circle and the square, pp. 107ff.

was observed.[65] As one of his own teachers explained, if you observe the back of a turtle, you will discover thirteen squares, one for each of the lunar months. Around these thirteen squares are twenty-eight smaller plates, one for each day of the moon's full cycle. Bruchac further explains that the four winds were given animal names to reinforce the Native American sense of oneness with nature. The north wind was called the "White Bear," the east wind, the "Moose," the south wind "Fawn," and the west, the "Panther." Bruchac's point, however, is that by observing the conditions of the natural world, Native American people were enabled to understand both the orderliness of the universe and those unique activities suited for human beings.

The number four is especially sacred to the Hopi people. Like the ancient Greeks, they also acknowledge a set of four basic elements: earth, water, wind, and life. Their legends are filled with fourfold themes. There are the four primary colors of the earth (yellow, red, white, and black), from which Spider Woman molded the four races of mankind; the famous four worlds; the four migrations; and the four sacred tablets.

From the four corners of the earth, one turns to the four winds of the earth in Mesopotamia epics. In the *Enuma Elish*, it is the four cosmic winds that assist in the creation of the earth. Like giant clouds of galatic energy, the winds of the four directions help Marduk overcome Tiamat and create life's massive building blocks amidst the spaces of night. Calling upon all the forces of the universe, Marduk strikes into the very soul of the monster Chaos, or the monster Tiamat. As a result, the universe comes forth, with all its stars, celestial fire, light, elements, and wriggling life.

> He then made a net to enfold Tiamat therein.
> The four winds he stationed that nothing of her might escape,
> The South Wind, the North Wind, the East Wind, the West
> Wind.
> Close to his side he held the net....
> He brought forth Imhullu "the Evil Wind," the Whirlwind, the
> Hurricane,

---

[65] See Joseph Bruchac's *Roots of Survival* (Golden, CO: Fulcrum Publishing, 1996), pp. 140-41.

The Fourfold Wind, the Sevenfold Wind, the Cyclone, the
Matchless Wind;
He sent forth the winds he had brought forth....
Her body was distended and her mouth was wide open....
He split her like a shellfish into two parts:
Half of her he set up and ceiled it as sky,
[The other half he made into earth].[66]

Hinduism displays a similar pattern. Here, too, we meet the
number "four" in the form of the four stages of life, the famous four
occupational divisions, the four Vedas, the four great cycles of time,
and the four paths of salvation. The four stages of life provide the
Hindu with proper signs, instructions, and rites of passage to guide him
from birth to death. The first is the student stage, the second that of the
householder, the third forest-dweller, the fourth the renouncer, or the
ascetic stage. The four occupational classes include the Brahmin, or
intellectual caste, the Kshatriyas, or military caste, the Vaisyas, or
merchant caste, and the Shudra, or workers caste. In time, the four
occupational classes became viewed as inheritable, the result of *karma*,
or the forces set in motion by one's previous life. The law of *karma*,
however, is a double-edged blessing, for it not only means that one's
present status is the result of one's past actions, but one's future state
can be altered by one's current actions and spiritual character. Thus one
can migrate upward, from a lower caste to a higher caste, until one
finally achieves *moksha*, or release from the cycles of rebirth. The four
Vedas represent the collected wisdom of the Hindu sages, which, in
time, led to the *Bhagavad-Gita* and its fourfold pathway of
enlightenment and peace.

Christianity has its twelve apostles, its four gospels, its four
liturgical colors (white, purple, red, and green), its four horsemen of the
Apocalypse, and its seven series of seven visions (the number "seven"
representing one phase of the moon), plus its seven sacraments. The
cross, however, constitutes the most remarkable repository of
quaternary phenomena. The four quadrants, the four cardinal directions,
the divisions between east and west, upper and lower, the vertical shaft
and the horizontal arm symbolizing the soaring eagle above and the tree
of life below, all converge here. How befitting that this ancient primal

---

[66] Pritchard, pp. 32ff.

cruciform should become the *locus sanctus* of the Son of God! Christianity also recognizes a spring equinox (Easter) and celebrates a winter solstice (Christmas). Above all, it honors its Virgin Mary, a figure as powerful and redemptive as any Ishtar, Isis, Asherah, or Mother Goddess of old.

> Hail, Mary, full of grace, the Lord is with thee. Blessed art thou among women and blessed is the fruit of thy womb. Holy Mary, Mother of God, pray for us sinners now and at the hour of our death. Amen.

There in a single credo is the earth, the womb, and the cycle of birth and death.

Even the give and take of Yang-Yin, the struggle of opposites in Taoism, is a form of the cyclical view of life. For everything there is a season: a time to be passive and a time to be assertive, a time to blend in and a time to stand out, a time to flow like a stream and a time to rage like a river, a time for firecrackers and a time for the butterfly, a time for the cherry blossom and a time for the snow.

Humanity's heritage belongs to us all. Its sense of being encompassed by an Eternal Power or an Eternal Thou never fades.

"Great Grandfather, all over the earth the faces of living things are all alike."

Chapter 20

The Anasazi of the American Southwest and the Hopi Worldview

The spirituality of the land of the American southwest has been acknowledged for centuries. From the time of the Anasazi (the Ancient Ones) to their descendants today, the Hopi, Zuni, and other Pueblo people, its earth and sky have been cherished. One cannot travel long in the Four Corners region without sharing a similar feeling of wonder. The immeasurable openness of land and sky, of mountain and prairie, elicits it from you.

From Santa Fe to Bernalillo, New Mexico, the clean, clear vistas of rolling desert tug at your soul. The August sky has cleared of thunderstorms. Everywhere the land is alive. Mounds of dark green juniper dot the landscape. Shades of sage stretch in every direction. Even the Rio Grande runs swift and deep near the ancient ceremonial chambers (kivas) of the Coronado State Monument. Here, in a tiny museum beside the dusty ruins of the pueblo Kuaua, some of the earliest murals of the Anasazi may still be seen. The faded colors and primitive figures can only hint at the complexity of the Anasazi legends, preserved in mythic code on these walls.

As one journeys north the green floor of the desert yields to the multi-colored hues of standstone that rise all around. The depths of the earth lift to meet the traveler in the rusty reds and ashen tints of the high plateau.

Just to the west, in the Chaco Canyon, spiral petroglyphs of circles within circles enabled the Ancient Ones to observe changing solstice and equinox with devotion and gratitude. Mother Earth. Father Sky. One stands amid the wind-swept pueblos, humbled and awed by the pink and gray colors of the ragged ruins. According to Navajo legend, it was here in Chaco Canyon that Nohoilpi, the trickster gambler, was placed in a bow and shot up, up, and up, until he disappeared into the sky. When the god who ferries the moon finally sent him back to earth, he fell to the ground in Mexico, where he became the "ruler" of the Mexicans, the ancient enemy of the Navajos.[67]

At Farmington, Alice Anne and I welcome the evening to a long and dusty day. Here the Animus River rushes past the willows and cottonwoods, creating bands of fertile oases between the white bluffs. The rocks along its banks are smooth; in the dusk, its waters tumble a metallic white. The sound of its passing washes through the soul, cleansing the spirit.

The next day, the long climb to Mesa Verde draws us slowly into the sky. Atop its magnificent "green table," one can see the La Plata range to the northeast and the distant, snow-laced peaks of the Rockies. In the steep canyons of the mesa's cliffs, the Anasazi built their pueblos of rose-brick homes, tucking each under an overhanging ledge or natural dome. Father Sky. Mother Earth. Each alcove of pueblos with its kivas. Each kiva a sacred home for honoring the Creator and the Spirits that bless the earth.

By the time one arrives at the Canyon de Chelly, one's heart is racing to catch up with all the splendor one has seen. How to store it all is a marvel for memory to master. Everywhere the vastness of the landscape, the hues of the sandstone, the sheer walls of the canyons, streaked with manganese varnish and swaths of purple cobalt, the angular patterns of black ravens drifting overhead, and the ever-stirring wind in the pines, works its miracle of silencing the noise within. The Buddha emptiness, the healing Tao is all about. "Be still and know that I am God," the ancient Israelite's heart would have whispered to his soul.

Finally, we arrive at the First Mesa of the Hopi nation. We drive to the top and park our car in the crowded square where tourists congregate. We are led by a Hopi woman through the narrow streets of ancient Walpi. Not founded until 1417, time has been kind to this superbly preserved pueblo. I can still see its mud plastered houses and the gray stones of its streets, the cottonwood logs and willow thatches that are used to support its archways. Precipitous cliffs fall away on

---

[67] Locke, op. cit., p. 85.

three sides. Steep, narrow stairways lead down to the desert floor. To the north, at the base of the mesa, one can see the corn rows and plots of squash and beans that help sustain the village's inhabitants. We drive on to the Second Mesa and from there to the Third and to the most revered of all the Hopi villages, Oraibi. We have reached the farthest most point of our planned tour. Now time and memory must assimilate what the eyes of the heart have seen.

As we fly out of Albuquerque, I glance down at the Sandia mountain range below. I can see the pinyon pines and sandy soil along the mountain's pink crest. A lone, dusty road makes its way to the top. Off to the south, the land ebbs endlessly toward the horizon. The sun is bright. Hey, hey! It is a good day to be alive. To affirm the mystery of one's existence. But my heart is sinking fast, for I hate to leave this place of striking vistas, filled with its ancient ruins and sacred silence. But it is time to return. Time to go home to South Carolina. And to the sound of the Chattooga, and the shade of the hemlock and the laurel. And the paths I love to walk.

Reference has already been called to the fourfold nature of Hopi beliefs. This fourfold pattern of the cardinal directions, however, can hardly do justice to the fascinating cosmology of their worldview.

According to ancient legend, the Hopi people entered the present and Fourth World at a sacred location in the Grand Canyon region, near the confluence of the Colorado and Little Colorado rivers. They emerged through a *sipápuni,* or hole in the ground. From this *axis mundi,* or "center of the universe," they began their legendary migrations, which would take them to the four corners of the Americas.

After centuries of wandering, the clans reunited in the high mesa country of northeastern Arizona. There appears to be no single definitive tradition concerning the origin of these clans,[68] but, apparently, from the south came the Side Corn, Parrot, Sand, Tobacco, and other clans. From the north came the Bear, Bluebird, Spruce,

---

[68] Anthropologists and historians differ as to the origin of the Hopi as well as the meaning of their treasured legends. Throughout this chapter, I rely on Frank Water's *Book of the Hopi* (New York: Penguin Books, 1977) for the information I provide. A highly resourceful and more popular account may be found in Robert L. Casey's *Journey to the High Southwest* (Chester, Conn.: The Globe Pequot Press, 1990).

Snake, Horn, and Flute clans. From the west, the Fire, Water, and Coyote clans, and from the east still other groups. Based on the bright birdlike colors that appear in the ceremonies of these people, as well as their language, scholars conjecture that the members of the Hopi clans were associated with the Uto-Aztecan people of Mexico, or Central America.

The earliest settlements of these Ancient Ones may well have been prior to A.D. 700. By 1150, Oraibi was established on the Third Mesa. As other clans completed their migrations, villages spread to the Second and First Mesa. By the time the Spanish arrived in 1540, the Hopi constituted a proud and ancient people, whose forebears appear to have been the cliff-dwellers of Chaco Canyon, Mesa Verde, and the Canyon de Chelly.

The worldview that came to dominate in this high mesa country has been described as esoteric and mystical, intricate, if not, impenetrable. Upon closer examination, however, their vision has preserved one of humankind's profoundest understandings of its linkage with the cosmic and regenerative forces of nature that not only make life human but also give it hope and direction.

Ancient Hopi legends trace the beginning of the universe to Taiowa. Taiowa, the Creator, represents that infinite, immeasurable void that can never be pinned down. He is the "I am who I am" of the Hopi, their Tao, or their "ground of being," in Tillich's words. Taiowa created his nephew Sótuknang to make manifest all that was potential in Taiowa. In obedience to his uncle, the nephew created the nine kingdoms (inspired by the nine stars in Corona), the seven universes (based on the seven stars of the Pleiades), and the primary elements: earth, water, wind, and life. Sótuknang entered the first universe, or First World, and created Spider Woman, who in turn created the twins Paqánghoya and Palöngawhoya, who keep the earth spinning on its axis. Spider Woman then created the earth's plants, animals, and the first humans, whom she molded from the earth's yellow, red, white, and black soils. Sótuknang was pleased with Spider Woman's work and blessed each human color group with a distinct language. Then he commanded them: "I have given you this world to live on and to be happy. There is only one thing I ask of you. To respect the Creator at all times. Wisdom, harmony, and respect for the love of the Creator who made you. May it grow and never be forgotten among you as long as you live."[69]

As the first humans matured, they thought of the earth as a living entity, as their Mother, and of the corn also as a living entity. They perceived their Mother in a dual aspect, as Mother Earth and the Corn Mother. They also knew their Father under two aspects: as the Sun in its vivifying powers, and in its brilliance they saw the face of Taiowa, their Creator.

Frank Waters, in his commentary *Book of the Hopi* compares their understanding of human nature to Tibetan and Hindu forms of mysticism. All three forms of mysticism posit a series of psychophysical centers, in which psychic and bodily functions unite to keep humanity human and open to its highest possibilities. All three views postulate that along the axis of the spinal column run several vibratory channels or centers. The Hopi acknowledge five. The first of these centers lies at the top of the head--the soft spot at birth--or the "open door" that makes communication with Taiowa possible. At death, the soul will depart through this opening. This opening also accounts for "out-of-body" experiences. The second center is the brain. By means of mankind's rational capacity, one can serve the Creator with obedience and respect. The third sphere centers about the throat, breath, and breathing. By means of this vital force, humanity can sing praises to the Creator and chant his holy name. The heart constitutes the fourth center. From a good heart flow good actions, from an evil heart, evil. It is the karma of the Hopi. The last sphere is the navel, the solar plexus, the throne of the Creator.

In this First World of endless time and endless space, the first people were pure and happy.

As time elapsed, the descendants of the First People used their vital forces (pranas in Hinduism) to advance themselves. They forgot or ignored the admonitions of Sótuknang and Spider Woman. Their language and color differences became barriers for further separation. Even the animals withdrew from them, as they did from Enkidu in *The Epic of Gilgamesh*. The people quarreled and went to war. Taiowa was saddened by these events (much as Yahweh was saddened by Noah's generation) and ordered his nephew to save as many faithful people as possible and to destroy the First World. Sótuknang gathered the "elect"

---

[69] Waters, p. 7.

and led them to the Ant People, where he hid them in the Ant Kiva. He then destroyed the First World with fire. The ancestors of the Hopi learned a valuable lesson, however, while staying with the Ant People: how to keep cool when it is hot and warm when it is cold, and how to live peacefully as a colony, in obedience to the Creator's plan.

After creating the Second World, Sótuknang rapped on the door of the Ant Kiva. He was welcomed and entered (just as the *kachinas* [spirits] are welcomed today, as they descend into the Hopi kivas to initiate the sacred ceremonies). Sótuknang thanked the Ant People and sent humanity on its way. He reminded them of their created purpose-- to respect the Creator and his plan for life.

Once again, as time passed, humanity quarreled, divided, and split. Once more, Taiowa ordered his nephew to gather the faithful, destroy the Second World, and create a third. Sótuknang called anew upon the Ant People to protect Taiowa's true believers, then he destroyed the Second World by means of ice.

In time, a Third World was created. It, too, had to be destroyed, but this time by a flood. Legend depicts the faithful journeying eastward across a sea, the islands of their refuge sinking behind them, one after the other, until they arrive on their reed boats to a new land, the Fourth World. Here each group was commanded to follow its "own star," until it had compeleted its unique migration. In this new world, humanity discovered a new deity, Másaw, Taiowa's appointed guardian of the Fourth World. Másaw reminded mankind of its ancient duty: to remember the Creator and to obey his laws. If they failed to do so, then he would have to intervene and rule the earth it their stead. Thus began their migrations.

As Waters points out, even a casual reader can detect a conflict of traditions here. Waters prefers the journey motif, which brought the Hopi's ancestors ashore somewhere in Central America. But the *sipápuni* legend is equally revered, and both traditions have been blended and preserved. Equally phenomenal is the subconscious memory of violent fires (volcanoes?), the Ice Age, the Mesopotamian myth of the great flood, the sinking of a lost Atlantis, and the disappearance of previous times, worlds, and cultures.

Upon their emergence or arrival in the Fourth World, a number of clans journeyed south. They were accompanied by *kachina* people. The kachina were not real people but spirits commissioned to help and guide the various clans. Somewhat like the brahmin caste of

Hinduism, the *kachinas'* purpose was to instruct the clans about their past and enlighten them as to how to fulfil the Creator's plan. The two most holy of the *kachinas* are Eototo of the Bear Clan and Áholi of the Water Clan.

According to one tradition, while journeying south, the Bear, Corn, Parrot, and Coyote clans were attacked by members of the Spider Clan. The latter were on the verge of prevailing when the *kachinas* intervened and helped the attacked clans escape. They did so through a tunnel that brought them north and into the Arizona area. It is for this reason that Hopi priests today wear the elaborate masks and costumes they do, in remembrance of the *kachina* people who taught them how to live and who rescued them from peril. By being faithful to this way of life, the *kachinas* bless and protect the Hopi clans, bring rain upon their parched lands, and sustain them year after year.

It is in the amalgam of this remembered "history" and prehistoric past that concepts of Father Sky and Mother Earth are blended to provide a foundation for the intricate ceremonies of the Hopi way. Winter and summer solstices and the fall equinox become the foci for the ceremonies that keep the Hopi faithful to their call. The ceremonies come in three patterns of three, like the three beads of the bright stars of Orion's belt.

The three great winter ceremonies celebrate the three phases at the dawn of creation. Wúwuchim in November is dedicated to the mystery of the germination of all living things. Soyál, the second ceremony, coincides with the winter solstice. Having reached the southern most end of its winter journey, the sun's return symbolizes the rebirth of life.[70] It signals an occasion for "silence, solemnity, and secrecy," writes Waters, for the rebirth of life must be paid for with life.[71] Soyál reminds the Hopi community of that archaic past when a young maiden was sacrificed during the winter solstice. As it begins its return, the sun also reminds the Hopi of the Creator, Taiowa, who smiles upon them through his winter face. The last phase of Creation is celebrated in late January and early February. It is called Powamu and means "purification." At Powamu, beans are planted and children are initiated into Hopi societies. It is a time for purifying the road of

---

[70] Much as the Christian Christmas (December 25) celebrates the birth of the Son of God.

[71] Waters, p. 157.

life each child must tread. As Waters explains, Wúwuchim, Soyál, and Powamu "are supremely dramatic interpreations of a creative plan whose power supersedes that of the limited human will."

The three summer ceremonies are Niman Kachina, the Flute and the Snake-Antelope ceremonies (the last two each appearing in alternate years). They commence at the time of the summer solstice, when seeds and fruits are in full flower and ripe. They signal a time for rendering praise to the *kachinas* for their role in blessing the earth's crops. At Niman Kachina, spruce boughs are gathered, placed in the kivas and blessed with smoke. The spruce is credited with a magnetic power to attract clouds and moisture. Eagles are also captured and sacrificed at Niman Kachina, as their feathers represent the power of prayer to rise upward and bear the Hopi's praise to life forms beyond the earth. The sacrifice of the eagles also symbolizes each Hopi's need to entertain good thoughts in order to promote the welfare of the earth.

The Flute ceremony takes place in late August. It comes at the time when corn, beans, melons, and squash are hardening. The rituals surrounding it serve a dual purpose: to help mature the crops by ushering in the last summer rains and to celebrate the Hopid emergence into the Fourth World.

Alternating every other year with the Flute ceremony, the Snake-Antelope ceremony likewise comes in late August. It too serves a double function: to summons forth the last rains of summer as well as celebrate the fruition of all life. The latter is centered about a ritual marriage between a young maiden of the Snake Clan and a youth of the Antelope Clan. The snake symbolizes the Mother Earth, the antelope the principle of fecundity. The ritual marriage represents the union of the great vital forces (pranas) that stimulate the physical and spiritual centers, thus enabling man to fulfil his highest function. As Waters puts it: "the Snake-Antelope ceremony cuts through the past to the ever-living now, and its stage is not the externalized universe but the subjective cosmos of man's own psyche."[72]

The final ceremonies occur in the fall. They are performed by the various women's societies. Known as Lakón, Márawu, and Owaqlt, they bring to conclusion the great cycle of seedtime and harvest, before another winter solstice returns. The full round of the seasons has been observed, Taiowa remembered throughout the year, and the value and

---

[72] Ibid., p. 238.

goodness of life reaffirmed. The nine festivals represent, what Waters calls, "a persistent faith in the multifold meaning of the Emergence."[73]

---

[73] Ibid.

Chapter 21

In Fields of Poppies

After completing my year at Villemétrie, I journeyed to Israel, under the auspices of a Swiss group: the Christian Movement For Peace. Our work-team was assigned to a kibbutz north of Haifa. I was the only American. The rest of the group consisted of Germans, Dutch, and Swiss, save for a young English girl, same age as mine.

I had been a faithful monk. Now it was time for me to enter the gates of manhood. I hungered for female attention, a young woman's touch. The English girl's name was Ida. Together we made the passage into adulthood. She was as passionate as I and equally shy and awkward. But together we discovered what to do and how to do it, and made love to each other, one star-bright night, on the edge of a wheat field.

When she left for Turkey, in late-April, my heart went with her. I would go out and sit beside the harvested wheat field and mourn her absence. I still remember her eyes, their sparkle that first night, her tiny breasts, and moist kisses. "For everything there is a season, and a time for every matter under heaven."

I stayed at the kibbutz a total of four months. During that time, the leaders of the kibbutz gave us two free tours of the country. The first was to the area of Galilee. I took many pictures, but I can still behold the land, as it was then. Ida was with me on both tours, but that was before we fell in love.

I can still see the green hills above the Sea of Galilee, the blue sky, the fields of red poppies, the white buildings of Tiberias tucked against the slope. Across the sea, rose the Golan Heights with its winding road that gleamed silver in the morning sun. To the north was the old synagogue at Capernaum, and to the east, Ida and I watched the sea oats bend in the evening breeze on the lake's windward shore. Later we visited the remains of Ahab's stone chariot stalls at Hazor, where the snow-covered summit of Syria's Mt. Hermon guards the valley to the north. In both ancient times and then, the valley glistened with sheathes of new wheat, waving in the wind. I stood there for a long time at Hazor, searching the mountain peak. It was on its icy slopes that Jesus was "transfigured" before his disciples, and along its shoulders that Tiglath-pileser III's army pushed its way south to conquer the Israelites in 733 B.C. Sennacherib's army followed the same route; so also Nebuchadrezzar's. Even pharaoh Neco's expedition had made its way north along the same path in 609 B.C. Alexander came by ship. But not the Seleucids who tried to Hellenize the Jews in the mid-second century. They too came down the valley, right past the chariot stalls. And centuries and centuries earlier, descendants of *Homo erectus* had come this way, but journeying northward instead.

The second tour brought us to Mt. Carmel, Jerusalem, the Negev, Solomon's mines and the sea at Aqabah. It was cold when we arrived in Jerusalem, for it had snowed the afternoon we had driven up from Tel Aviv. Later, during graduate studies, when I began exploring the books of the Apocrypha for the first time, I would remember that afternoon. Chapter 13 of 1 Maccabees records the story of Simon's attempt to rescue Jonathan from Trypho's army. The two armies had been moving parallel to each other and were in the vicinity of Jerusalem. Trypho wanted to attack. Simon wanted to rescue his brother. It began to snow. The snow fell deep and soft and Trypho cancelled his attack and pushed his army across the Jordan to Gilead, where he killed Jonathan. I could imagine Jonathan, bundled in his thin cloak, watching the crystals descend, as Trypho turned his army away from Jerusalem. And from Simon.

The weather moderated as we descended toward the Negev, though the nights remained cold. We slept beside the lorrie at night. It was warmer in the plain of Arabah, and when we arrived at the Red Sea, Ida and I took off our shoes and waded out into the water. The beach was pebbly and the tiny rocks were red and worn smooth. That night we camped beside the lorrie along the coast. Not a single building or condominium was in sight. As we lay there, we could watch the lights twinkling across the bay in Elath.

I remember the festival of Purim, the beer, wine, and dancing; the courtyard of flowers and willow trees outside the dining room; the cry of jackals at dusk; the patrol that slipped out every night, machine guns slung across their shoulders, to take up vigil behind the barbed-wire along the hilltops; the sea wall at Caesarea; the shops of Tel Aviv; the locusts, heat, and rope-climb up Masada.

In May I crossed into Jordan through the Mandlebaum Gate in the back seat of an embassy car. In my right hand I clutched a folded affidavit that proclaimed to all the world that I was an official U.S. citizen, who had "misplaced" his passport. The affidavit was stamped with the U.S. seal. The Jordanian border guard stopped the car, peered inside, then waved us through. I was in the Hashemite Kingdom of Jordan, in the ancient walled city of Jerusalem, in the land of Moriah where Yahweh had commanded Abraham to offer Isaac as a sacrifice. I was in the land of Mohammad, where Crusaders had died in the name of the Cross.

I stayed at the American School of Oriental Research. During the month and a half I boarded there, I toured all the ancient places on the West Bank, Ajlun and Gerash in the Jordanian hills, Qumran, the Dead Sea, and Petra, the fabled kingdom of the Nabataeans.

By late June I was eager to return home. I had traveled enough. It was time to be a student again, to return to the seminary. I felt I could take it, whatever the "it" was.

I remember going down to the suq one last time, past the Turkish tobacco shops, the Wailing Wall, the Temple area to stare east toward the Mt. of Olives. The week before I had taken a bus to Bethany to see the ruins of Lazarus, Mary, and Martha's house. Then I had climbed the Mount of Olives to rest at its summit and gaze one more time across the Kidron at the city's ancient towers, its walls, and the Dome of the Rock. A beggar from Bethany had followed me half way up, begging for pennies. I had given him none. Finally, he sat on a rock and began to cry. "Please, just one." But beggars are legion in the Holy Land, and I was young and had had my fill. So I walked on.

That night, back in my room, I read Mark 14, a passage that narrates Jesus' last visit to Bethany. My heart fell into the pit of my stomach as I read the Son of Galilee's words: "For you always have the poor with you, and whenever you will, you can do good to them." Early the next morning I returned to Bethany, but the beggar was gone.

Chapter 22

The Separation of Essence from Existence

When did the phenomenon of the shattering of our affinity with nature arise? At what point did Western humanity conclude that its *essence* was other than its *existence*? When did we cease to see ourselves as conscious extensions of the elemental forces of the universe, of star debris and cosmic gases, of soil and sea, or sentient partners with all other life forms in the biotic community, and, instead, see ourselves as qualitatively distinct from all other life forms, with a destiny that stretches into eternity? And ours superior?

By the time of the great pyramids the threshold had been crossed. That its dawn may precede the fertility figurines and cave paintings of Cro-Magnon Man seems likely. But its rapid development from the time of Homer on is a fact. Both Socrates and Plato witness to this "advance." Humanity had come to see itself as possessing two lives: an outward, corporeal, public, and historical life, versus an inward, spiritual, private, and contemplative life, the latter being superior to the former and capable of immortality.

The meaning of this "advance" is clear. The separation of the soul from the body had occurred. Increasingly, over the next millennium and a half, soul and body would be viewed as antithetical. The age of alienation had begun and, with it, humanity's quest for wholeness again.

For Martin Heidegger, this is the central problem of philosophy. What is Being and how do we listen to the voice of Being so as to overcome the alienation that sours in our hearts?

Throughout the mountains of Western North Carolina there are rivers that run deep and green and plummet swiftly past steep banks of rhododendron. Some flow toward the distant Tennessee; others spill through gorges and cascade down the cliffs along the North Carolina-South Carolina escarpment. The Broad River is the mightiest of these and flows eastward through the midlands of South Carolina.

The Chattooga, the Whitewater, the Thompson, the Horsepasture, and the Toxaway are smaller, but each has coursed its way over the escarpment and down the face of time, creating spectactular waterfalls along the way. But falls abound everywhere, filling the heart with their soft rumble and the patter of their flow.

Here *essence* and *existence* are one and the voice of Being clear, as the drone of the river envelopes the forest, the hemlocks, and the pine.

It is a Taoist wonderland of opposites in unity, a Zen realm of weathered stone and coursing streams, pine litter and mossy trails, the slumbering grounds of the morning sun on its journey west toward the sacred hills of *Wakan Tanka*.

In his own search for unity, Nietzsche turned to the symbolism of Apollo and Dionysus for illumination. *The Birth of Tragedy* is the title under which he records his search. For Neitzsche, Aeschylus and Sophocles were the best Greek playwrights because they understood how shadowy and fate-driven human existence can be. Euripides, on the other hand, interjects too much order and reflection, thus undermining the tragic dimensions of life.

The Greek tragedies were a function of the tumultuous festivities and orgies that centered about Dionysus, god of the vine and immortality. Nietzsche seizes upon this symbolism and sees Dionysus as the gateway to intoxication, creativity, passion, spirit, frenzy, and all the hidden primal instincts. Apollo represents the phenomenon of light, illumination, order, balance, serenity, and form. Apollo ultimately triumphed in Greek society, thanks in part to the achievements of Socrates and Plato, who were devotees of order. The cost, however, was tragic, for Dionysus was dethroned. Consequently, humanity's darker urges were consigned to oblivion, regarded as inappropriate and inferior to Plato's eternal forms, with their power to lure us upward. The age of alienation had walked boldly on stage. The god of the vine was forced to retreat. The ground for the Christian faith was laid.

Nietzsche's interpretation deserves respect, for his analysis of Apollo and Dionysus has profound merit for our self-understanding. In Nietzsche's view, we are driven by both Apollinian and Dionysian urges. We cannot understand ourselves apart from either pole. Our essence lies in a unity of the two opposites.

Upon closer examination, Nietzsche's philosophical-psychological evaluation of the human condition is not dissimilar from the Sioux Indian's worldview. The latter's spirit and passion for the earth and sense of relatedness to all living things is the Dionysian side of Lakota religion. Whereas, its endorsement of bravery, endurance, generosity, and wisdom reflects its drive toward order and illumination, symbolized by its acknowledgment of the *tunkashila*, the Creator, the Great Grandfather, or the Apollinian dimension in Nietzschean thought.

So too in the case of ancient Israel. Consider again its metaphors of image, dust, and breath. Humanity is created in the "image of God," out of the dust of the Mother Earth, but ennobled by the life-giving breath of Yahweh, the Father God. What is remarkable is that the ancient Israelite never panted after deification, or elevated his contemplative and rational capacity above his earthly and corporeal nature. He never imagined that he would survive death, nor did he care to. He was content to return to the dust and yield his spirit, his *ru'ah*, to the holy mystery that empowered his fragile existence. "Into thy hands I commend my spirit." One life was sufficient, one journey lived in gratitude to God. *Einmal und nicht mehr.*

We have much to learn from these two cultures and the *Vorstellungen* they use to interpret mankind's affinity with the elemental forces of the universe and his place amidst the biotic community of Eden, or the lush plains and sacred ground of the Black Hills. Theirs is the insight of reverence for life, a journey never to be repeated on this earth, ending in the holiness of death, with the release of the human spirit. Giving and taking, they accept the flow of life.

I would like to think that such a view as theirs has the capacity to lift us beyond the lingering dogmas that sometimes leave us empty and, in its way, survives Descartes' principle of "radical doubt." René Descartes (1596-1650) longed for a philosophy founded on self-evident truth and called upon his era to subject everything else to radical questioning. Hemingway encouraged the same in his quest for a "built-in, shock-proof, shit-detector."

If religion is to survive, it must celebrate anew our affinity with the earth, reunite soul and body, discard doctrines that are incompatible with what we know to be true about the universe, and assist its adherents to rediscover the art and joy of living. Such a program neither requires nor condones the wholesale rejection of the world's great religious traditions. Rather, it encourages us to review religion's time-honored insights and our *human* responses to the "divine mystery" and numerous sacred experiences of mankind. Then, perhaps, we can hear once again the voice of Being, with hearts humble before the mystery of existence. "If we have listening ears," wrote Gandhi, "God speaks to us in our own language, whatever that language be."[74]

---

[74] *The Words of Gandhi*, selected by Richard Attenborough (New York: Newmarket Press, 1982), p. 74.

Chapter 23

Theophanies, Sacred Texts, and Religious Language

Theologians contend that if religion were nothing more than each individual's experience of the infinite within, then nothing objective or universal could be said about religious experience or God. Religion would become little more than each human being's quiet adjustment to his or her inner loneliness and sense of wonder before the universe. Such a possibility frightens the orthodox of most faiths. Nonetheless, it is a legitimate objection.

Certainly, Karl Barth was uncomfortable with such an approach. For Barth, there is a qualitative distinction between time and eternity, the finite and the infinite. No amount of self-exploration on our part can disclose the true nature of the divine. God must do that for us. God must take the initiative. God must come to us.

Reihold Niebuhr espoused a similar view. In his *Nature and Destiny of Man*, Niebuhr argued that only a "religion of revelation" can do justice to humanity's nature, in which the transcendence of God is preserved.[75] Otherwise, God is swallowed up by mysticism. For Niebuhr, God is more transcendent than "the eternity of mystical faith." As Niebuhr explains, the danger of mysticism lies in the human tendency to equate the "final depth of human consciousness" with some ontological level in God.[76] That is, mysticism believes that if one explores one's own being deeply enough, one will come to know God

---

[75] Niebuhr, p. 126.
[76] Ibid.

in some redemptive way. But, to Niebuhr's mind, this equating of the self with God fails to take human pride, alienation, and the limits of human freedom seriously enough. This results in the loss of God's mercy that sets humanity free from its delusions and despair.

Tillich, in part, concurred with Niebuhr and Barth. Though he still favored his ontological approach, Tillich maintains that we are aware of the Infinite within, not only because of its inescapable presence, but also because of the phenomenon of "revelation."[77]

For Tillich, revelation involves "mystery" and "ecstasy." By mystery, Tillich means "the mystery of mysteries." Mystery has to do with the ground of existence, the depth and essence of life, the ultimate beyond which no one can go. When this mystery is unveiled, without losing its mysterious and essential nature, then we understand what life is about. "Ecstasy" is derived from the Greek word *exstasis*, which means to stand outside oneself and see the world as one has never seen it before. Ecstasy is not the negation of reason, but its fulfillment. It can also come as a shock. Thus revelation occurs when the mystery of mysteries is experienced in such a way that the veil is removed and we understand what life is truly about.

Other scholars refer to these revelatory moments as *theophanic*, or as constituting *hierophanies.* Theophanies and hierophanies mean that a manifestation of the divine (*theos*) or the holy (*hiero*) has occurred, and that the recipient of this experience knows himself or herself to be in the presence of the ultimate mystery or the transcendent God. According to this view, genuine hierophanies are unsolicited and occur because the holy manifests itself.

Sacred texts and sacred scriptures contain records of these ancient theophanous encounters. They preserve the supreme, hierophanic moments that certain prophets, prophetesses, holy men, and others experienced. In the Old Testament, it is Moses who comes to mind and his theophanic moment in the Sinai desert, in which Yahweh's self-revelation overwhelmed him, causing the patriarch to bow before the phenomenon of the "fire," both in the wadi and in his heart. He was never the same afterwards. In the East, it is the Buddha who attracts our attention, who, seated in meditation, was suddenly

---

[77] See Tillich's, *The Dynamics of Faith* (New York: Harper Torchbooks, 1957), pp. 3-16; 76-79; also his *Systematic Theology*, Vol. 1 (Chicago: The University of Chicago Press, 1951), pp. 106-118.

seized by his revelation concerning suffering. He too was never the same afterwards, but it led to his vision of the Eightfold Path, which still enlightens followers worldwide.

Sacred scriptures, however, are more than anthologies containing theophanous encounters. They are also the products of history, culture, and unique languages. They trace the story of those ancient persons who first cherished the original insights, "revealed" to them in their respective time and place. In the Old Testament, it is not uncommon for the prophets to acknowledge that their oracles are educed insights, based on a "word of Yahweh" that they have *"seen"* (Amos 1:1). Like poetic utterances, their oracles are meant to inspire us with creative glimpses of what could be, if only our hearts were open to the holy and the good. The same phenomenon underlies the insights of the Buddha, the Hindu sages, the koan of Zen masters, and the visions of Native American medicine men.

Religious language constitutes a discipline of study in itself. How are these scriptures to be interpreted? What is the function of their language? Are they describing something that is empirically true about the universe, that actually adds to our knowledge of the universe? Or are they offering an insight as to how to live *now*, on the earth?

Philosophers of religion tend to endorese the second alternative. In my own estimation, the American philosopher John H. Randall, Jr. (1899-1980) provides one of the keenest analyses. In his *The Role of Knowledge in Western Religion*, Randall proposes that religious statements have nothing to do with explaining the universe. Science does that. Nor do religious statements provide supplementary information that adds to the truths of science. Simply put, religious beliefs cannot generate any knowledge about the universe, for that is not their purpose. Religious beliefs are symbolic, imaginative, and figurative ways of conceiving of our relation to the "nature of things." As such, they do not represent or explain external things. Instead, they act on our wills. They produce results in our conduct and activity. They provoke common responses; inspire insight and vision. They help us unify our experiences and interpret our lives.

The human mind, however, is very restless and demands to know more. How are we to distinguish between these beliefs? it asks. Aren't some of them *prima facie* more valuable than others? Don't some of the views and statements even conflict with the beliefs of other traditions? Aren't we obligated to be discerning and critical? The answer, of course, is yes, but that does not imply that one tradition alone is right and the others all false. The wisest position may well be the one that John Hick commends as "pluralism" and which he defines as follows: "the view that the great world faiths embody different perceptions and conceptions of ... the real or the Ultimate from within the major variant cultural ways of being human."[78] In spite of the differences, however, Hick notes that each religious tradition affirms that "there is a limitlessly greater and higher Reality beyond or within us," and that this "Reality exceeds the reach of our earthly speech and thought."[79] For Hick and others, whether we call that Reality "God," "Nature," or the "Tao," seems less important than its meaningful impact on our lives.

In the final analysis, perhaps Gandhi said it best:

> I believe in the fundamental truth of all great religions of the world. I believe that they are all God-given and I believe that they were necessary for the people to whom these religions were revealed. And I believe that if only we could all of us read the scriptures of the followers of these faiths, we should find that they were at the bottom all one and were all helpful to one another.[80]

---

[78] Hick, op. cit., p. 425.

[79] Ibid., p. 427.

[80] *Gandhi*, p. 78.

Chapter 24

The Umbrian Hills

Sometime in late June of 1961 I boarded a plane at the airport in Nablus for the flight to Athens and the beginning of the long journey home.

A sadness now crept inside, for I felt very much alone. There was no American School of Oriental Research to return to, no shaded courtyard for escape from the heat, no tea served in the late afternoons, no kibbutz, no work-team, no Ida to love or be loved by. I thought of her. Her hair, her eyes, her kisses; her presence at my side. I so much wanted her just then. She had left without leaving a single forwarding address. I supposed that she had crossed the Ukraine, perhaps had stopped in Prague, and was now in England. I never heard from her or saw her again.

After visiting the Acropolis, the Parthenon, the Areopagus, and the ancient stage where Dionysus had died to the crowd's clamor for a new wine, I left for Venice. I booked passage on a small liner that passed through the Isthmus of Corinth, stopped at the Island of Corfu, and then sailed into the blue waters of the Adriatic.

Venice brought me back to life. But what I remember most is not so much the food and wine, or the traditional places: the Doges Palace, the Bridge of Sighs, the Grand Canal, St. Mark's courtyard and Cathedral, the latter crowned with its bronze equistrian statuary stolen from Constantinople. No. What I remember is a piece of art and a moment of silence. It was a painting in the Museum of Fine Arts that captured my attention as I walked through a narrow portal.

It is a large painting by Bonafacio de Pitate in which he captures something of the awe of Luke's story of the Annunciation. It is a dynamic thing, for it evokes a profound silence from you and creates a feeling that somehow the Holy is real and that the momentousness of God is astir. That you are in the presence of the Being of Being. That the Infinite God of the universe exists.

The scene is late evening. Low hills trail off to the left of the canvas. They are obscured in the shadows of large clouds, massed into thunderheads, pregnant with power. Only a thin wedge of light between the hills and clouds separates the night from the last gray cry of day.

At the bottom of the picture lies a town, shuttered-in behind its pale walls, with the exception of a light that breaks through an open window where a young woman, aroused by the rumble of thunder, or perhaps a voice, stands cautiously, anticipatingly, looking out into the night.

Gabriel has come, come from the presence of God, to this lonely town, with a message that will change the world. His great wings hold him in the process of lighting, one foot already on the patio. His head is in profile, his face turned heavenward, conveying the feeling that even he is overwhelmed by the message that he has been commissioned to announce.

No Christmastide has come and past that I do not remember Pitate's painting.

From Venice I took the train to Florence. I loved its square, its cathedrals, its statue of David, its rivers, bridges, and Uffizi gallery. There was a tall girl at the youth hostel who caught my eye. She had long black hair, a sensuous body, and a thin but pretty face. Her eyelashes were long and her breasts protruded from under her blouse. She was Italian and enjoyed laughing with me, but she was traveling with a big Swede. He kept pulling on her belt.

"You watch where your eyes go," he said to me.

Later I met a little German girl. She had bright green eyes and dark red hair and was prettier than the Italian. She would have "counted coup" with me, but at the time I was still in love with Ida. We stayed up all night and had breakfast together. She kissed me good-bye, before departing for Innsbruck that morning. I walked down to the train station with her and watched her board.

After Florence, I hitchhiked up into the Umbrian Mountains to visit Perugia and Assisi. I loved both towns and stayed three days in each. I can still see the monastery on the hill, the dirt square, Giotto's paintings. The death scene of St. Francis. The eyes, the faces, the hands. The place where icons died and humanity was reborn in art. I visited it every day I was there.

I loved the mountains as well. The vineyards, the hills, the olive trees, the little towns, the hamlets, and villas; the inns beside the road where you expected to find none. I lunched in one, relishing every piece of bread I dipped into the salad and especially the morsel I used to sop up the last beads of oil and vinegar. I wanted to stay longer, but I had exhausted my hostel limit of three nights in one place.

Finally, I arrived in Rome. But like Luther of old, I was not impressed. In Luther's case, it was the paganization of the city under the Renaissance popes that shocked him. In my case, it was simple fatigue. Plus longing to get home. I was tired. Tired of so many sites, so many galleries, so many churches, so many hostels, so many ruins, so many everythings. I just wanted to stop, to listen, to look, to feel. To go back to Perugia and Assisi. And, yes, Villemétrie. I needed to withdraw again, reflect again, be alone, but in a community. But I was in Rome. And when would I ever come this way again? And so I toured the city, its fountains, Forum, the Colosseum, St. Peter's Basilica, the Sistine Chapel, and the art works of the Vatican. I enjoyed every minute of it, as tired as I was.

I was in that state of mind one morning, seated at a café, when a young paperboy came running by, with his newspapers under his arm, yelling, "*Hemingway e Muerto.*" My heart sank. I stopped the boy and bought a paper and read the story. I knew no Italian so to speak, but I was able to pick through the story and the account of Hemingway's suicide.

Hemingway was the reason I had come to Europe or had even wanted to travel. Apart from him I would have never come to France, for as much as anything, he was the cause of that restlessness that made the first year at Union so unbearable. Not that I wanted to be Hemingway. I wanted to be me, but in a way that could stand up to his detector. That is what I owed him, and my heart ached as I read the story. It still aches whenever I read him.

I journeyed on to Lurezia after that and rested there for several days. I stayed close by the bay and amused myself by swimming, drinking wine, and squirting lemon juice over the pink raw clams that were served in their black shells. In the evenings, I retired to the hostel that was housed in an old castle that overlooked the bay. I would sit outside in an iron chair and enjoy the breeze and watch the sunsets slowly grow scarlet across the sea. Then I would scoot down into my bunk and read from the Psalms and think about Hemingway.

I was a junior at Davidson when I read *A Farewell to Arms*. Its ending shattered any naivete I ever entertained about love or life or death. It took me months to absorb it. It was a watershed experience. As I lay there that night at Lurezia, I read and reread Psalm 139: "Even the dark is not darkness to Thee." More than ever, I wanted to return to Villemétrie.

I would go on to Pisa, Bern, Basel, Strasbourg, and Heidelberg, then, toward early August, I took the train for Paris and Villemétrie. All the brothers were glad to see me. André beamed and kissed me on the neck. He stood back and held my shoulders with his hands. "*Mes frères*. Look everyone. *Notre* Ben has become a man. It is in his eyes. *Voilà*, I see it now."

"It is good to be back," I said.

All of us went down to the canteen and André broke out a special bottle of wine.

"The Prodigal has come home," announced Pierre.

André filled our glasses and we clinked them together and toasted being good freres.

It was good to be back.

I wanted to visit Paris again, to see the Louvre one more time, its *Winged Victory of Samothrace*, *Venus de Milo*, and Rembrandt's *Bathsheba*. I loved Notre Dame as well, its rose windows and dark nave, its smoky vaults and votive candles flickering in the darkness in front of the Virgin's statue.

André graciously reincluded me in the *équipe*.

"*Voici ta blouse*," he smiled, as he handed me my old blue smock. It had been laundered and folded and was in a cabinet near the fireplace. "Our new brother, Albert, is the chauffeur, but you can be of help to Pierrot, until your voyage. *D'accord?*"

"*Oui*. I'll enjoy working with Pierre in the garden. I've always loved the earth. *La terre*."

"Good."

The last week of August the air turned cold. I had to wear a sweater on walks in the park. There was a grassy clearing under an old oak that looked out over the wall at the east end of the estate. The ivy had been cleared from the yellow stones and one could sit on the chalky wall and look out across the silvery orchards toward the olive-green hills of La Ferté-Alais.

They reminded me of the low mountains on the long drive to Spain that a seminary friend and I had taken the previous August, before I dropped him off at Montpellier. There he would study as an exchange student for the year. I was to meet him at Le Havre for the return voyage home. But just then my memory was filled with San Sebastian, its long gray curve of beach, and the soft lights that stretched out of sight at night around the bay. I could see the high mountains on the way to Burgos, the flocks of sheep and lone Basque herders; the cathedral of Burgos itself, its stark walls and the town's narrow streets. Then came the dry valleys and white hills on the way to Madrid; the Prado and its paintings by El Greco, Goya, and Velásquez; the plaza de toros and the bullfights I watched and the tall matador who killed his bull with a single thrust of the sword. I can still see him in his gold-braided suit, his black cap and black slippers, the veronicas he performed with his red cape, and the glint of his steel sword.

Hemingway was dead. As I sat there on the wall, my imagination fell sway to the ancient Tempter of old. I could feel his presence. His cold breath on my neck. The wind stirred. His lips parted.

So ... your Hemingway is dead. What will you do now?

I will go back to America.

But is your heart in it, señor? Is your heart truly in this thing you must do?

I have my gift. And you know what it is? And the Giver who gave it?

Ah, your gift! And your Giver! So you think that will do? This gift you have? You should accept mine, and be done with it all.

It is the Giver who has given me my gift. I have had it since childhood. It was given to my grandmother first. And she passed it on to me.

And that will do, this gift of yours?

Yes. I am confident.

Very well, señor. But if you ask me, it is a strange gift. This gift of yours.
    No stranger than the Giver.
    Ah, touché! Your heart is set on it, isn't it?
    Yes. Sometimes there are things we must do alone. They are deep in our hearts, where no one can see. But we know they are there. And that we have to do them.

    The night before my departure, André proposed that I drive the *deux-chevaux* to the train station the next morning and that later in the day he would ride down on his bicycle to drive it back.
    I rose early before dawn, carried my dufflebag out to the vehicle and placed it in the rear compartment. After relatching the doors, I walked to the driver's side to get in. I glanced about the old chateau one last time. The red geraniums and dark green ivy were barely detectable in the pale light. The courtyard was cold and a thin white mist drifted through the open gates.
    Just then André stepped out on the stoop at the top of the bannistered stairs. He had a commanding way of standing at attention with his eyes riveted forward and his hands clasped calmly in front of him in meditative fashion. He was wearing his blue blouse and baggy trousers. His white hair was uncombed and his glasses were pushed back on his forehead. He stood in silence, looking out across the courtyard toward me.
    I stood beside the vehicle and brought myself to silent attention and beheld the man.
    Moments later he quietly stepped back inside and stood by the window.
    I got in the *deux-chevaux* and drove through the gates and up the narrow street through our tiny village and passed the sugar-beet fields beyond. The sun was just then beginning to come up and its rays bathed the walls of the on-coming village a dull yellow, then orange and bright lemon. I drove past wall after wall, through village after village, past tobacco and beer advertisement signs, until I came over the long rise that dropped suddenly toward the train station. I parked in the parking lot, dragged out my dufflebag, dropped the keys in the front seat, and bought my ticket and waited in the cold air for the morning train that would take me to Paris. There I would change trains for the ride to Le Havre and the voyage home.

Sometimes in the early morning when I stand on my deck alone I see André again, standing there in silence, reminding me who I am and of the gift that life's Giver has given me. For the Giver never leaves anyone giftless, he said. Isn't that so, *tunkashila*?

Chapter 25

Eden in Paris

In the winter of 1970 I returned to France. André was no longer associated with Villemétrie but had opened a new front as an itinerant evangelist and guest lecturer of the Reformed Church of France.

My wife Margaret and I were living in Paris. We were both studying French at the *Alliance Française* and on the weekends were taking the train to Villemétrie, for me to research its published bulletins and determine if the idea of a "Protestant monastery" might work in the states. Our study was funded through the Rockefeller Foundation. André was off somewhere in Stassbourg or *le Midi*, and the staff at Villemétrie did not have access to his itinerary or know of his address.

Paris was very cold that winter and Margaret and I spent hours walking the boulevards, sitting in cafés, and touring museums, just to keep warm. We stayed in a pension off Rue D'Assas, just opposite the Garden of Luxembourg. Our room was on the fifth floor and its radiators seldom worked. Finally, toward spring, the weather turned warm and the city's parks and tree-lined boulevards beckoned to us from every quarter.

The war in Vietnam was very intense just then, and there were many North Vietnamese "students" in Paris, whose sole purpose seemed to be to propangandize Americans abroad. Once, for a two-week period, I could not walk through the garden without being invited "to sit and talk" with one of these Vietnamese. The editor of the anti-war magazine *Ramparts* was also in Paris, along with scores of hippies.

The hippies were everywhere in the Latin quarter. It was rumored that the CIA had its operatives among the group and that one needed to be careful with whom one spoke. I attended a rally, sponsored by *Ramparts*, but came away with ambivalent feelings. After all, I wanted our country to "win" the war, though later I would change my mind. As a young pastor in Franklin, Virginia, I had driven down to Norfolk for my physical, with the intention of volunteering as an army chaplain. But the recruiting officer took me to one side. "Reverend, you're past the age limit by one year. Your chances of being sent to Nam are nil. Besides, the whole damn thing will be over in a few more months." That was in 1966. "If you've got anything better to do, don't go."

The music "A Whiter Shade of Pale" had just been released in Paris and was very popular, and wherever Margaret and I went, we heard it being played. It became "our song," part of our journey.

Paris grows on one, and we were no exception. Every afternoon, we looked forward to having tea and a tart at some sidewalk café or a crêpe in one of the parks. We whiled away hours at the Louvre and were blessed to be in Paris at a time when the city sponsored a special exhibition of Chagal's works. When not at Villemétrie, we worshiped at the cathedral of Saint Sulpice, where the people were warm and friendly and the priest's homilies were simple and unaffected. Then on those Sunday afternoons, we would make the long walk to Notre Dame to hear the organ recitals presented there during the winter months.

The windows of our room opened onto the Rue D'Assas. From our tiny balcony we could see the *hôtel américan*, where prostitutes in fur coats lined up at the corner of the Rue Bréa to ply their trade. No one seemed to mind their presence and male passersby often tipped their caps or berets. On a nearby sidestreet a disco proudly advertised "*les plus beaux transvestites du monde.*"

One weekend, while at Villemétrie, I was informed that André was in Paris. I was given a telephone number and could hardly wait to return to the pension to call him. He was not present, but the *concierge* took my message and assured me that she would relay my wishes to "*le bon pasteur.*" André finally telephoned, and I invited him to the pension for lunch.

He arrived, looking none the worse for the passing of a decade. Beneath his overcoat, he was clad in a blue sweater, white shirt, and gray tie. He kissed my neck and enfolded Margaret's hands in his own. "*Le plaisir c'est à moi*," he smiled.

While we were dining, I learned where he was bound to next.

"You know the story of my life? The bishop of the Catholic diocese of my first parish? *Alors!* he's a dean at the Cathedral of Notre Dame. I'm to have dinner with him this evening. After all these years! *Mais* we have been friends for a long time. Then it's off to Belgium."

I walked with him to the metro. We shook hands. "The Lord be with you." "And with thee," I replied. He smiled, his eyes bright, a true conduit of the depth of the ground of Being, of the kindness of God in his heart. Then he descended the tiled-stairwell to catch the subway.

There is a time to embrace and a time to say good-bye. A time to keep and a time to cast away. A time to have and to hold, and a time to let go. The journey of life includes many polarities. They are part of its passage and flow. And many of them are painful.

Margaret and I are no longer married. But there were many "embracings" before our "good-bye," before we "let go." We have two sons who forever link us to each other and to the heart of the earth's creative powers.

Transitions are never without anguish. They too are part of the journey of life, part of its flow. They are part of the challenge of passageways. Who has not observed them in nature, or in the stories of others? The rites of passage take on a strange meaning when they apply to you. They cease to be abstract and become personal. They are part of life, though not everyone experiences the same kind of passages. They too belong to the earth and our finitude, even part of its spirituality. And the ones we don't anticipate are the most demanding. Yet to make peace with them is part of the challenge. Karl Jaspers refers to them as "boundary situations." The journey of life suddenly brings you to a boundary. Death is the greatest boundary, but so also is divorce, and any form of guilt and remorse. All choices and risks involve boundaries. But boundaries carry a hidden possibility as well as an inner dread. And in that lies their spirituality. For they offer an opportunity for a new being to emerge, a second chance to reassess one's life and experience "an authentic" existence. As Jesus put it to Nicodemus: "Do not be astonished that I said to you, 'You must be born from above.'" The boundary provides an opportunity to wake up. It is a form of grace. In that sense, it comes to us as undeserved.

"Lord, remember me when you come in your kingdom," the one thief asked. "Today, you will be with me in paradise," the dying Savior replied. And, so, transitions occur, and thanks to caring friends, I met Alice Anne, and remarried.

Somethings remain indelible, even for us "the most fleeting of all." And among them is love and its power to renew our lives. It is a facet of the mystery of our finitude. Little wonder that the ancient Greeks, as well as the Canaanites and Assyrians, extolled their goddesses of love and family, fertility and regeneration. For such giving and bonding is of the essence of the earth. Even the New Testament anchors humanity and sexuality, the human need for community and one another, in the deepest mystery of which it knows. For "God is love, and those who abide in love abide in God, and God abides in them" (1 John 4:16). As human beings we may mirror the mystery imperfectly, but to love and be loved is inseparable from our *ru'ah* as well as our dust. It constitutes the profoundest mystery of the earth and of ourselves as manifestations of the mystery of being.

Chapter 26

Rain and the Mystery of Being

Light rain and drizzle possess cathartic power. Their arrival is an invitation to relax our pace. To welcome them is to open ourselves to those multi-tiered levels of our own psychosphere, where memory and reflection work their healing powers. From the shelter of the inner self, the heart discovers anew the primacy of its own existence and the wonder of Being itself.

One can imagine our Pleistocene ancestors, huddled in caves, watching the rain. Ever alert to the sounds of its patter, their instincts respond to every movement and shadow that waxes and wanes in the mists.

It rained a lot that winter in Paris. The rain was often raw and cold. Once it snowed. I happened to be along the Quai à France, near the Pont Royal, staring across the Seine toward the Tuileries. The river ran high and swift. Slowly it began to turn white. Flecks of snow floated by in tiny armadas of bobbing flotsam. I had not realized how choked the river was with submerged debris until it snowed.

I thought of Ezra Pound's "Portrait d'une Femme."

> Your mind and you are our Sargasso Sea,...
> In the slow float of different light and deep,
> No! there is nothing! In the whole and all,
> Nothing that is quite your own.
>   Yet this is you.

Nature's misty days draw out the "slow ... deep" of our own Sargasso Sea. As it rises within us, it releases memory and reflection to cast their spell of "different light" on who we are. Such moments bring us into the realm of the transcendent.

I remember a snowfall one winter in Michigan. It was on a weekend. It was dusk. Our group of scouts was struggling its way through deep drifts along a trail bordered by white pines, whose boughs were heavy with snow. Suddenly a large owl swooped down upon us, then fanned its wings desperately to climb the barrier of pines and disappeared into the darkness and the falling snow.

Time after time that scene returns to me. Frost writes:

> The winter owl banked just in time...
> And her wings straining suddenly aspread
> Caught color from the last of evening red.

In still another poem, "Auspex," he describes the "eagle bird in all its terror" that swooped down upon him when he was small but elected not to strike. His family offered comfort and explanation. But he concluded:

> I have remained resentful to this day
> When any but myself presumed to say
> That there was anything I couldn't be.

Reflection has a way of bringing us into consciousness. And consciousness in turn brings us before the infinite and the question within ourselves. "What is it? What is it all for?" "The owl of Minerva spreads its wings only after the falling of dusk," Hegel observed.

That snow and rain, drizzle and river, owl and pine, shadow and dusk should put the question to us is entirely natural. Indeed, the *ru'ah* within ourselves forces us to ask the question. It is an inescapable part of life's spirituality.

Among early Christian philosophers, no one understood this better than Saint Augustine.[81] Listen as the question comes back to him in his own encounter with the earth.

> I asked the earth.... I asked the sea and the deeps and the creeping things, and they replied, "Seek above us." I asked the fleeting winds,... the whole air ... the heavens, the sun, moon, and stars; and they answered, "Neither are we ... whom you seek..." Is not this beauty of form visible to all whose senses are unimpaired? Animals, both small and great, see it but they are unable to interrogate its meaning. But man can interrogate it.... See ... what a condition I am in! Weep with me, and weep for me,... But do thou ... give ear; look and see, and have mercy upon me; and heal me--thou, in whose sight I am become an enigma to myself.[82]

The rain, the mist, the snow. The flowing stream. The trees, the breeze, the mountain peak. The sun, the moon, the dome of stars. Always and ever anon the question comes back to us. And only you can answer the question for yourself.

André Malraux, one of Charles de Gaulle's ministers of culture during the years of the Fifth Republic, approached life's spirituality with profound candor. In his book *Anti-Memoirs*, Malraux notes that the greatest mystery underlying our humanity is not that we have "been flung at random between the profusion of matter and stars," but that within ourselves we can draw upon "images powerful enough to deny our nothingness." He goes on to quote his Uncle Walter: "Something eternal lives in man--in thinking man. Something that I would call his divine self: his capacity to call the world in question."[83]

Malraux was a tank commander in World War II. In 1944 he was captured by the Germans and held overnight in a convent at Villefranche-de-Rouerque. At dawn he was to be executed. As he

---

[81] Saint Augustine (354-430), a Christian theologian and bishop of the North African city of Hippo. His work has enjoyed an enduring influence on Christian thought. He is remembered most notably for his *Confessions* and the *City of God*.

[82] See Augustine's *Confessions*, Library of Christian Classics (Philadelphia:Westminster Press, 1955), pp. 206-231.

[83] See Malraux, *Anti-Memoirs* (New York: Holt, Rinehart and Winston, 1968), pp. 24-28.

awaited the coming morn, he requested a Bible. Left alone in his cell he turned to John's Gospel in preparation of his death. That night American forces rumbled into Villefranche and the German Wehrmacht withdrew. Later, when Malraux was writing his memoirs, he reflected on that evening and his reading of John's Gospel. He concluded that the "genius of Christianity" is that it proclaims "that the path to the deepest mystery is the path of love, ... a love that transcends" humanity "like the soul of the world," more powerful than death or justice.[84] It is his phrase "soul of the world" that sums up the depth of that Presence that lies at the heart of one's experience with the earth.

In his book *Out of My Life and Thought*, Albert Schweitzer reflects on his own encounter with Being and the many questions his soul was forced to raise. It became Schweitzer's conviction that the universe itself "is unable to give the final answer to the great question of what we are ... and to what purpose we exist." We can find that answer only to the extent that we "experience ... the universal life which wills and rules within." Such understanding only comes "through the living Being which is within."[85]

He explains how the concept of "reverence for life" occurred to him. His missionary party was making its way up the Ogowé River. Their boat had been chugging along for three days. It was at sunset. The river was clogged with lumbering hippotamuses. The behemoths filled the river and were crowded onto a sandbar. They appeared pink in the fading light of day. Suddenly, "there flashed upon my mind, unforeseen and unsought, the phrase, 'Reverence for Life.'"[86] Schweitzer mulled the scene over and concluded: "Man does not simply accept his existence as something given, but experiences it as something unfathomably mysterious."[87]

That is what makes us human and what so many cultures, for all their variations, have tried to say. It haunts the center of our existence, and explains, in its mystical way, why we are attracted to both science and religion, nature and transcendence.

---

[84] Ibid., p. 155.
[85] Albert Schweitzer, *Out of My Life and Thought* (New York: Holt, Rinehart and Winston, 1958), p. 105.
[86] Ibid., p. 156.
[87] Ibid., p. 158.

Part III: The Voice of Being Speaks Many

Languages

Chapter 27

A Philosophical Repertoire

As the years have passed, a select repertoire of philosophical stories and insights continues to survive Hemingway's detector. Each has the capacity to help us rediscover the importance of ideas and their power to illumine the question of existence.

The first is Plato's "Allegory of the Cave." You will find it in Book VII of the *Republic*. It begins with the words: "Let me show in a figure how far our nature is enlightened or unenlightened," and it goes on to depict humanity as a band of prisoners, bound side-by-side in a cave. All they can see are the shadows of objects cast on the screen of their cave. What they cannot see are the objects themselves, or the fire whose light makes the shadows possible. Only after one of them has been unchained and "compelled to stand up and turn his neck around" does he begin the journey of shedding illusions for reality. The sad irony is that Plato (428-348 B.C.) himself surrendered as illusion that Dionysian dimension of our humanity that can be so creative, while encouraging his fellow Athenians to aspire for something higher. But the truth of Plato's allegory remains.

All of us have settled for shadows in some form or other. That is why Descartes was right to launch his adventure for "clear and distinct" ideas that could survive "radical doubt" and free one from misconceptions. The world had lived long enough under the shadow of Medieval authority, and he wanted to question everything afresh. It was the impulse behind Hemingway's dream of creating a genre of fiction that would transcend falsehood and, in turn, open both the writer and the reader to the truth of the moment and its capacity to empower our lives.

Such a search for the "moment of truth," or "the-thing-in-itself," has never been without cost. In Plato's story, the enlightened prisoner must once again descend to the world of the prison-house to awaken as many others as he can. As Nietzsche puts it, the highest goal of humanity "is the pain of telling the truth." Only when that occurs can "men transform their lives."[88]

It is difficult to find, let alone "tell," the truth. If we take Barth's approach, it is only when the Infinite God descends to the finite and touches and moves our hearts that we are able to know that we are in the presence of truth. Even then, for Barth, it is not so much an abstract truth that God offers us, but the Holy Reality of God Himself, a Reality that transcends all "truth," and which can never be captured or pinned down by words. If we take Tillich's "ontological approach," which was also St. Augustine's and Plato's, then the reality of the Infinite is already within us. We are already in the presence of the Eternal Now, of "the ground of being." Its tug on our souls and sensibilities is inescapable. As Hinduism proclaims: "That Self is thyself. That thou art." Brahman is within. Or as the Buddhists explain, we are already one with the Buddha essence; it is only a matter of our "waking up" to see it. Black Elk endorsed a similar view: "All over the earth the faces of living things are all alike."

Not only is there pain in telling the truth, but there is also pain in accepting the truth. We have come from dust and will return to dust and our breath will return to the universe. Accepting this truth is painful, while at the same time it transcends the painful, because it is truthful. It undergirds our "dignity," as self-transcendent beings, as well as preserving our "humility," as evolved creatures of the earth. Accepting this truth makes it possible for us to be open to the voice of Being and, therefore, to the myriad possibilities that Being provides.

There is a Zen poem that sends its arrow straight to the target.

> Gateless is the Great Tao,
> There are thousands of ways to it.
> If you pass through this barrier,

---

[88] See Geoffrey Clive, *The Philosophy of Nietzsche* (New York: New American Library, 1965), pp. 348-50.

You may walk freely in the universe.[89]

Plato is only one of many places to begin.

His student Aristotle (384-322 B.C.) offered an observation as profound as any embedded in the "Allegory of the Cave." Writes Aristotle: "For one swallow does not make a spring, nor does one sunny day; one day or a short time does not make a man blessed and happy."[90] Aristotle believed that humanity's highest goal requires "virtuous activity." To achieve this goal, one must learn to do "the right thing at the right time in the right manner for the right reason." This takes a lifetime to achieve. It was Aristotle's way of acknowledging that life is a process, a journey, and that inculcating virtues that grow out of character is no easy matter. "For the things which we have to learn before we can do them we learn by doing;...men become just by the practice of just actions, self-controlled by exercising self-control; and courageous by performing acts of courage."[91] How can it be otherwise?

For Aristotle, the process of life requires *patience, action, and vision.* All three are requisites. *Patience,* because we do not know how to act justly except in the practice of acting justly, or how to act bravely, or with kindness, or tolerance, except in the same way. *Action,* because if we never put into practice our choices, ideals, or dreams, life sours from inactivity, from a profound, unrequited, unactualized sense of *transcendence,* which leads to despair. It is the misuse of that sacred gift that the universe and the Giver has given everyone. And *vision,* because without the latter, our patience and actions are misdirected and blind. In that sense, Niebuhr is right: "The meaning of life is more than the living of life." It requires time, wisdom, action, openness, humility, grace. It demands a linkage with a vision that both transcends and pervades our sense of self. That is why Aristotle's thought is so keen. It is what Gabriel Marcel means when he writes:

---

[89] See *Zen Comments on the Mumonkan* by Zenkei Shibayama (New York: New American Library, 1974), p. 14.

[90] See Martin Ostwald, trans., *Aristotle: Nicomachean Ethics* (New York: Macmillan Publishing Co., Library of the Liberal Arts, 1962), p.17f.

[91] Ibid., p. 34.

A man cannot be free or remain free, except in the degree to
which he remains linked with that which transcends him....
When I myself speak here of a recourse to the transcendent, I
mean ... a level of being, an order of the spirit, which is also
the level and order of grace, of mercy, of charity.[92]

As an aside, it is of interest to note that the Plains Indian still
practices a rite known as the "vision quest"--the *hanbleceya*. For four
days the participant enters a pit in the Mother Earth. Surrounded by
total darkness, he is forced to withdraw deeper and deeper in the self.
There all his demons and illusions are released to fade away. He must
now behold with his heart what his eyes cannot see. With his soul
freed from all distractions, he awaits the coming of the Spirit. He
becomes one with the earth. There in the silence of the Void, he opens
his heart to the Mystery of Being. Visions occur. New strength is
given. New directions take wing for life's journey.

It was in a quiet wadi on Mt. Sinai that Moses beheld the
"fire" of God and was given a vision that transformed his ancestors'
faith into a living religion, zealous for justice and hope. It was in a
cave on Mt. Horeb that Elijah received a similar vision "in the still
small voice" that redeemed him from self-pity and called him to action
again. And it was in his own *hanbleceya*, in the cave of Mt. Hira, that
Mohammad received his visions, through the voice of Gabriel, who
whispered Allah's truth in his ears.

The Mother Earth in her capacity as Mediatrix enabled each to
experience anew that "order of the spirit" that rekindles human hope.
Even the Essenes withdrew into caves, as did Nietzsche's Zarathustra.

Epictetus (60-117) represents a third line of thought, equal to
Descartes' principle. It has to do with his phrase "things in our power"
versus "things not in our power." His Stoicism of the second-century
A.D. has many valuable features. One must not grieve over facets of
life that are beyond one's "power." Nothing is gained by a will that
succumbs to life's defeats. At the same time, reason discerns that there
are many things that are within the human purview. These we must
have the will to change or to act upon, or, indeed, we will lapse into an
inauthentic existence. It is his Stoic vision that empowers the

---

[92] Gabriel Marcel, *Man Against Mass Society*, cited by Robert Solomon in
Existentialism (New York: Modern Library, 1974), p.131.

philosophy underlying the famous Serenity prayer: "God grant me the serenity to accept the things I cannot change, the courage to change the things I can, and the wisdom to know the difference."

Epictetus's is an interesting vision, in spite of the fact that at times it collapses into fatalism. Nonetheless, his favorite *metaphors* for illustrating his views draw on the motif of the journey and the mysterious Agent-Director behind and within the universe. Call it karma or nature; it is one and the same. To that extent, his vision is modern and shared by other traditions. When you are on a voyage and your ship puts into anchorage and you disembark, never wander too far from the ship, for you never know when the Helmsman may call, he advises. So it is in life.

Interpret this any way you will, but life is a journey and will move on--with or without you. You can live in the past, run from the ship, or hide from the Helmsman, but life is going to move forward. How much wiser to understand this and maximize conditions as they are. If there is something to be done, some dream to be dared, actualize it now, for the Helmsman is coming. If there is something to be "let go," let go of it now. Be ready, alert, warned Jesus, for you do not know at what hour the Bridegroom may come.

"Ask not that events should happen as you will, but let your will be that events should happen as they do, and you shall have peace" (*The Manual of Epictetus*). The sting of the razor's edge clings to this entry, but we know that there are times when its truth applies to all humanity.

Anicius Manlius Severinus Boethius (480-524) also deserves mention. His *Consolation of Philosophy* is still worth reading. He wrote the *Consolation* while in prison, awaiting his death. Separated from his library, he consoled himself with a synthesis he had been developing throughout his life. He believed that man was more than Aristotle's mortal, "rational creature," and that somehow our human freedom is bounded by an Infinite will that gives depth and purpose to our lives, but one that refrains from interfering in the flow of our lives. "If you spread your sails for the wind, you must go where the wind takes you." With Aristotle, he recognized that there is a natural dimension to human life, the pursuit of which yields profound satisfaction. But, in keeping with the biblical insight of the "image of God" motif, man is also a transcendent creature, whose capacity to rise above the self imposes a self-concept that requires reflection. "For the nature of man is such that he is better than other things only when he knows himself, and yet if he ceases to know himself he is made lower than the brutes."

One could devote a chapter to the problem of universals that dominated discussions throughout the Middle Ages. Do any of our concepts equate with anything out there in the universe? Or are they only convenient names for describing our thoughts and experiences? The problem easily goes back to prehistoric man, who sat mesmerized in front of his fire, haunted by the images that danced in his mind. Just what is the nature of concepts? How "real" are they? Do our concepts point to a reality that transcends them, or are they only abstractions of our human reflection, as finite and time-bound as we? Indeed, does not all language have about it the character of Hegel's *Vorstellungen*, those picturesque words, that we are forced to use in order to grapple with our experiences? If such is the case, then doesn't that make all our language of art, religion, and philosophy all the more dear, as well as our hypotheses of science? We can say nothing "objective" that is not already the result of our "subjective" encounter with reality. In the final analysis, life is not only a *journey*, but a form of *response* in which we acknowledge the givenness of the universe, our unique place in it, as well as our finitude. That is why Black Elk's prayer to the *tunkashila*, the Great Grandfather, is so powerful, as well as the Buddha's self-emptying silence, or the Son of Galilee's prayer in Gethsemane. They are "subjective" responses to the "objective" reality of the universe, in which our capacity for self-transcendence requires us to turn toward the Infinite, however one is compelled to define it. Peace of heart cannot come until we are at peace in our minds and hearts with the universe.

George Berkeley's (1685-1753) response in the eighteenth century still evokes wonder, if not cynicism. *Esse est percipi* is the phrase he used. "To be is to be perceived." And since the universe is always being perceived by its Giver, it exists. Make what you wish of it, but the unperceived, the never conceived, or the unacknowledged, has no power or meaning to direct our journey, until we wake up and "see" it. This is as true of the forest wanderer, the hiker of trails by falls, as it is of the scientist in the field or lab. "Concepts without percepts are empty and percepts without concepts are blind," is the way Kant put it.

Immanuel Kant's (1724-1804) Copernican revolution in philosophy created a stir that still unnerves the world. The astronomer Copernicus (1473-1543) had theorized correctly that, rather than the sun orbiting the earth, it is the earth that orbits the sun. Copernicus's ideas stunned a dogmatic era that thought that the earth was actually the center of the universe, as the Christian faith seemed to imply. The Church fought Copernicus's ideas, because it foresaw that both God and the earth would be marginalized, if the Polish astronomer were right. Kant seized upon this insight and applied it to reason, concluding that it is not so much that our ideas conform to the world as the world conforms to the operations of our minds. He divided knowledge into two categories: *Verstand* (reason) and *Sinnlichkeit* (sensible knowledge). The former represents the way our minds think. They cannot help but impose order, quality, and unity upon our experiences. The latter represents what is known by our five senses: sight, sound, touch, taste, smell. Still, when *Verstand* and *Sinnlichkeit* are combined, all we can know are phenomena, things as they appear to us. We can never know noumena, things as they are in themselves. Since "God," the "self," and the "world" are "concepts" that cannot really be known through our sense perceptors, Kant referred to them as "transcendental ideals." We can postulate them, but we cannot know that they exist in the way that we can "perceive" phenomena. As erudite as his thinking is, on reflection, his system is bounded by the earth. Both *ru'ah* and dust are facets of the earth, which we can never transcend except in the form of "postulates." It is a humbling philosophy that recognizes our finitude and the finite quality of our best reasoning. And yet it is Kant, the supreme philosopher of the Enlightenment, who turns his heart toward the Infinite, with openness and humility, and without fear of censure says: "two things fill the mind with ever new and increasing admiration and awe ... the starry heavens above and the moral law within." He gave his heart to the Being of Being and listened to it with all his powers.

I have already drawn upon Hegel (1770-1831). He created a great synthesis of Being. In it the Absolute unfolds itself in the historical drama of life, in which its secrets are discernible to philosophers in the form of concepts. The latter give rise to the motifs of history, which we see enacted before our very eyes. Then we watch as these great life-forces take new forms as they are expanded by resistance, and finally remolded to form a new synthesis. His ideas both spellbound and drew criticism from his contemporaries. His insights live on and his analysis of art, religion, and history is particularly resourceful. But one post-Hegelian, in particular, reacted with defiance.

His name is Soren Kierkegaard (1813-1855) and the theme he advanced was revolutionary: "The particular is higher than the universal," the individual higher than the ethical. Conservative minds are still shocked by any espousal of this view.

In his book on logic, Aristotle argued that what is true of the universal will be true of the particular; however, the converse is false. We cannot go from the particular to the universal. He reasoned that once we have identified the *archai* of any given class of entities, we may then attribute to its particular members those characteristics that are true of the class as a whole. This reasoning gives abstract concepts a higher value than the particular tangible entities, which mirror them in a flawed way. Hegel endorsed this system, subjugating the particular to the universal, exalting the more objective forms of Spirit (e.g. the state) over the individual.

Kierkegaard could not abide this reasoning as true, at least, for human beings. The particular, the individual, and the value of an individual life, carries more weight than abstractions. The prime example of this is the story of Abraham, who must suspend the ethical, that is, transcend the universal law of not harming his son, in order to meet God's test.[93] In Genesis 22:1-20, God requires the patriarch to sacrifice his only son Isaac in order to prove to himself that he, Abraham, puts God above all other relations. God demands an absolute relationship that transcends universal generalizations. God places more value on Abraham's particular response than on any system of universal "truths" that pertain to all humanity. God demands a passionate response, as subjective and particular as each human life is, and without any guarantees. Abraham does not know in advance how the trek to Moriah will turn out. He does not know what awaits him at the end of the journey. He only knows that God demands absolute allegiance. And in his painful embrace of the Unknown that will not let him go, he finds freedom.

Kierkegaard goes on to distinguish between the "tragic hero," whose life never transcends the parameters of the universal, and the "knight of faith," who risks all by his "leap of faith" and passionate

---

[93] See Kierkegaard's *Fear and Trembling*, trans. by Walter Lowrie (Garden City, New York; Doubleday Anchor Books, 1954).

commitment to "God." Only the "knight of faith" will experience an authentic existence, however filled with anxiety and pain. The only alternatives are twofold: become an *aesthete* who never commits the self to anything, or an *ethical person*, who abandons one's unique individuality to endorse the world's codes of ethics at large.

The Buddhist in his self-imposed silence, the Lakota in prayer to the *tunkashila,* obedient to the *Wakan Tanka,* the Hindu sadhu meditating in his ashram or in crusade for Hindu rights, the Christian in prayer to Jesus or Mary, and the man or woman of science, obedient to the voice of Being that lures them, are all acting upon this Kierkegaardian insight. The individual is higher than the universal, the particular more important than any ethical, religious, or philosophical system. We must each make our peace with the universe from which we have come and which pulsates within us as well as the mystery to which our breath belongs. You may think of that mystery as the Allower of myriad *Vorstellungen,* of many varied views, or simply as the Silence within the Big Bang. Either way a leap of faith is required, a reverence for life, and the realization that "all over the earth the faces of living things are all alike." That, too, is part of the homeward journey. If not its heart.

In an earlier chapter we reflected on the separation of the soul from the body and the tearing asunder of one's essence from one's existence that such a separation invites. In the twentieth century, a number of philosophers have explored this split, but none has done so with as much imagination as Gilbert Ryle (1900-1976), who taught at Magdalen College, Oxford. Ryle has attempted to solve the problem by dissolving it. For Ryle, the mind and the body are not two separate *substances*, or two different *species* of existence; rather they represent two different *senses* of existing. To dissolve the problem, Ryle offers three distinctions. He 1) analyzes what he calls the "official doctrine," 2) criticizes its "absurdity," and 3) investigates what he calls "the origin of the category-mistake."[94]

He dubs the "official doctrine" the "dogma of the ghost in the machine." It states that we have a body and a mind. The body occupies space and is subject to spatial laws. The body has a public, observable history. It forms one's physical world. The mind is not in space or governed by mechanical laws. Its life is private, unobservable to the

---

[94] See Gilbert Ryle, *The Concept of the Mind.*

outsider, and comprises one's mental world. Thus, a person has both a physical and a mental life, or a physical and mental history. At death, the physical world and history perish, but the mental life goes on.

Ryle finds this doctrine absurd. It is the result of a "category-mistake." It assumes that the mental life constitutes a separate category of existence, different from the physical life. But actually we enjoy only one phenomenon of existing. Mind and body constitute a unity, which "indicates" two different senses of existence, but not two separate substances.

What is the origin of this mistake? Descartes, who thought of matter as an entity of mass in space and in motion and subject to the mechanical laws of nature, versus the mind which is not in space or subject to mechanical operations. Consequently, he postulated two separate substances, two different species of being. But, of course, he in turn was drawing upon the split between mind and body that can be traced to Socrates and Plato.

Ryle's analysis is powerful, uniting mind and body in a single acting being, and not too dissimilar from the ancient Israelite's vision of humankind as a unity of "dust" and "spirit," in one living soul. His is an engaging interpretation of our humanity as a being of the earth, in which both our "dignity" and "earthliness" require address, but within the bounds of a scientific reasonableness.

Finally we come to Camus (1913-1960) and his *Myth of Sisyphus*. To be certain, there are others to be read. Unamuno and his *Tragic Sense of Life*; Dostoyevsky's *Notes from Underground* and his *Brothers Karamazov*; Tolstoy's *Death of Ivan Ilyich*. But it is Sisyphus who most commands our attention. For he is a true exemplar of the earth. Condemned by the gods, his fate was to roll a stone to the top of a mountain every day, where upon it would roll back down in the evening, and he would have to repeat this feat day-after-day, throughout eternity. For Camus, Sisyphus symbolizes the truth of our human condition. It is without meaning, an absurdity. We long for meaning, but life has no meaning, other than the meaning we give it. There is no God behind the universe, or force within nature providing direction, encouragement, or illumination. We are on our own; there is no outside consolation on which we can draw. You must draw it from within. You must have the courage to accept this absurdity, defy it, and, in community with all other humans like yourself, carve out a world of meaning that transcends despair. There is a humility and honesty about Camus that is very appealing. Why not accept it and stop here?

Perhaps the only answer that adequately addresses this question is the answer the cavemen gave in the legacy of their art, or the Buddha experienced in meditation, or the Lakota feels when he turns toward the sun, or Jesus incarnated in his very being. The voice of Being speaks many languages. Our very consciousness requires us to acknowledge the mystery of ourselves and the mystery of the earth's givenness. What is God? God is the manifestation of the mystery of our human condition. In experiencing the hollowness in his heart that hungered for meaning, Camus was responding to the voice of Being. Anyone who has ever read Camus' *The Plague* will recognize the Son of Galilee in Dr. Rieux.

To love the universe, the cosmos and the earth, and to recognize it in ourselves and others, is not an absurdity, but to acknowledge that we belong to *levels of Being* that have the capacity to humanize us and to satisfy the deepest recesses of our being, which includes the mystery of "relatedness" as well.

Chapter 28

The Many Faces of the Sacred

We think of masks as forms of concealment, or modes of disguise, that someone is hiding his true identity behind a mask. But what if that isn't the case at all? What if the mask is actually a conduit of revelation, a *Vorstellung*, a living manifestation of the most holy and sacred, but under the conditions of finitude? If that were the case, it would readily explain why the sacred so often comes to us in distorted, blurred, and unreal forms, tinged with elements of awe, and sometimes darkness and dread. For that is how we experience the sacred and both celebrate and preserve our memories of it. From that perspective, the Christ was such a mask, as well as the servant of Israel:

> there were many who were astonished at him
> so marred was his appearance beyond human semblance,
> and his form beyond that of mortals (Isaiah 52:14).

Sam D. Gill, a student of Native American traditions, argues that Native American masks served and still serve precisely this function. They manifest the sacred far more than they conceal it. Many of the faces are carved from tree trunks and, once carved, are considered to be alive. As Gill explains: "The full meaning is gained only by looking *through* the eyeholes of the mask," which only a society's members may wear, "and seeing the effect it has on the world."[95] Gill goes on to review the powerful role that masks play among the Seneca, the Kwakiutl of the Pacific Northwest, and the Hopi Kachina dancers. He concludes that what their masks symbolize is the living presence of the spirit world. Since we cannot fathom the depth of the holy, or plummet the sole of the sacred, the masks, at least, help us "experience" it as a reality.

I recall my own visit to a Mohawk shrine in Upstate New York and the black cloth drawn across the Iroquois masks, behind a display window. Here was a holy of holies, not to be lightly stared into by the carefree and the uninitiated. Of all the shrine's artifacts, the black drape, protecting the masks, alone survives to haunt and humble me. For what the masks proclaim is that we are more than dust and that we belong to forces and powers that struggle to shine through us, like fire dancing behind the eyehole-stars of the universe.

Paul Reps, in his classic collection of Zen writings entitled *Zen Flesh, Zen Bones,*[96] preserves a tale that carries profound meaning. It is the story of a woman who prized dearly her statue-image of the Buddha. She loved it so much that she overlaid it with gold. Daily, she prayed to the statue and burned incense in its presence. It was as dear to her as any rosary, or statue of the Virgin, or pocket-sized New Testament, is to a Christian. As time passed, she was forced to move. When she came to her new place of residence, she discovered a pagoda, devoted to the Buddha. It was filled with many gold statues and decorated with flowers. The smoke of incense drifted from its entrance; the presence of the Buddha, the silence of the Buddha essence, could be felt within. So she decided to deposit her image there, in a quiet corner of the pagoda. But after several visits, she became annoyed that the smoke from her candle tended to waft toward the other statues, so she made a little funnel that directed the fumes from her own incense straight onto her Buddha. This pleased her deeply, and she did it over a long period of time. One day, as she was kneeling before her image, she was shocked to detect how ugly her Buddha had become. Its nose was black with smoke, and it eyelids were covered with soot. Her Buddha had ceased to be handsome. The story does not tell us if she

---

[95] See Sam D. Gill, *Native American Religions* (Belmont, Calif.: Wadsworth Publishing Co., 1982), p. 71.

[96] Paul Reps, *Zen Flesh, Zen Bones* (New York: Anchor Books, 1989).

became enlightened, destroyed the funnel, or bowed in the presence of all the Buddhas, but I would like to think so.

Reps' collection also preserves the story of the famous Ryonen, a Japanese woman. She was young and wanted to become a nun, but she was very beautiful, and so her family dissuaded her. She acquiesced and married a wealthy prince, but on condition that after bearing three children, she would be allowed to leave the marriage to pursue her dream. Her husband lavished her with gifts and loved their connubial moments. But the hour came when she had fulfilled her promise and her husband had to let her go. Now she sought nunhood anew. But when she arrived at the first temple, the Zen master closed the gate on her, because she was too beautiful. The scenario was repeated elsewhere, again. What was she to do? She was determined to seek a higher beauty, to know a deeper satisfaction. She took a hot iron to her face, erasing her beauty forever. Then the master opened the gate, and she fulfilled her longing. "Whoever seeks to save his life will lose it, but whoever loses his life for my sake, will find it."

There is a similar version of this story in the *Gospel of Buddha* that is equally powerful. In it a young woman of beauty, a courtesan named Vasavadatta, has fallen in love with one of the Buddha's disciples, Upagutta. She invites him to visit her, but he replies that the time has not yet arrived for such a visit. She goes on to have affairs with several wealthy men, even having one of her lovers killed in order to make room for a more promising liaison. She is brought to trial, found guilty, and is condemned to lose her nose and ears, her hands and feet. Out of compassion, one of her maids cares for her. Finally, Upagutta visits her. Vasavadatta laments the loss of her beauty, but that is not why the disciple has come. "If I had come earlier, while you were still beautiful, then neither my words nor the Buddha's would have moved you. But there is a beauty that will not fade and if you can now accept the Buddha's teachings, you will find a peace that transcends life's cravings."[97]

My favorite involves a saintly man who saved his wealth in order to publish the first edition of the Buddha's sayings ever to be printed in Japanese. Just when he had enough to bring out the edition, a flood and famine struck, bringing disaster to many. Without

---

[97] Adapted from *The Gospel of Buddha* (New York: Open Court Publishing, Co., 1894, 1915).

hesitation, the man emptied his accounts to relieve the suffering. Once again he saved; he ordered the printers to begin the edition. But an epidemic broke out. Thousands were displaced. Misery lay everywhere. He ordered the printers to desist and dispersed his funds accordingly. Now he was old; little time remained. But once again he amassed the funds needed to bring out the edition. Finally, it was printed: a flawless collection of the Buddha's sayings, printed with wood blocks, seven thousand copies in number. It was then presented to the priest of a nearby shrine. He received it with gratitude, and to this day the edition can be seen in the Obaku monastery in Kyoto. But all who know the full story are fond of saying: "The first two editions were vastly superior."[98]

The Son of Galilee would have smiled. After all, was it not he who said, "Inasmuch as you have done it unto the least of these my brethern, you have done it unto me"?

Why are we afraid of the universe? Why are we afraid of each other? Why are we afraid of doing good? Why do we put dogma above our unity as people of the earth? Why do we hide behind any one religious tradition and close our hearts to others? Why do we close both our minds and hearts to what the world's finest scientists have to say about our universe, our planet, our human nature and destiny? How many bones of prehistoric man have to be unearthed before we finally realize that this time, and this time alone, is our time, our era, our moment, our epoch upon the earth? As the Buddha put it long ago: "The world does not know that we must all come to an end here. But for those who know it, their quarrels cease at once."[99]

Jesus was fond of saying: "Let him who has ears to hear, hear what the Spirit is saying." There is a directness about "truth" that can be missed with too much reflection. When the moment of truth occurs, one should act. Moreover, "truth" always escapes precise wording, for words tend to substitute for immediacy and action. We want time to deliberate, to mull over life before we commit ourselves. But sometimes that is fatal, and we postpone acting upon the moment of enlightenment that has come to us and sink anew into old patterns of inauthenticity.

---

[98] *Zen Flesh*, p. 36.
[99] From the *Dhammapada*, in Van Voorst, p. 91.

A scribe once blurted out to Jesus, "Teacher, I will follow you wherever you go." But Jesus replied that the Son of Man had no precise destination in mind, or place to "lay his head." He was simply in journey. Another said, "Let me first go bury my father, then I'll follow you, wherever." To which Jesus answered, "Follow me, and let the dead bury their own dead" (Matt. 8:20).

D. T. Suzuki, in his book *Zen and Japanese Culture*,[100] tells of a would-be student who wanted to learn the art of swordsmanship. So a master swordsman agreed to train him. But all the student did was tend the old man's garden, clean his house, and prepare meals. "That is not why I came here," the student grumbled. "Very well," answered the old man. From that moment on, the student knew no peace. Wherever he happened to be, the old man would suddenly appear and strike him with his stick. It took months for the youth to inculcate that sense of timing that enabled him to avoid the master's blow. It happened that the youth caught the old swordsman bent over a pot. Ah! Now was his chance. He crept quietly up behind the old fellow, raised his stick, and swung it down. But just as it neared the old man's head, the master turned and deflected it with the lid of his pot. At that very moment, the student received his enlightenment and thanked the old master for his patience and skill.

Jesus and the great teachers of the world rarely inudate their disciples with dogma. What they give us are *Vortstellungen*: pictures, stories, metaphors. And upon these we are encouraged to relate to the universe, its mystery, and to each other in ways that deepen our humanity. The "truths" of *Vorstellungen* may escape objective verification, but their veracity, reality, and insight are "experiential." Even Camus' Sisyphus is a *Vorstellung*.

Suzuki goes on to explain the meaning of one of Japan's oldest ceremonies--*Cha-No-Yu*: the Art of Tea. It is a ceremony in which two persons become one with themselves, each other, and the mystery of the earth and universe. The closest thing to it in North America is the Lakota Sun Dance and in the Chrisitan faith, the sacrament of the Lord's Supper or Mass.

Cha-No-Yu is a communion service. It is a profound ceremony by means of which persons come into harmony with nature

---

[100] D.T. Suzuki, *Zen and Japanese Culture* (Princeton: Princeton University Press, 1971).

and themselves. A number of components are required: a thatched roof over a small room, a running brook, nearby pines if possible, windows emitting only the softest of light, a fire under a crude iron kettle, water brought to a boil, then poured over ground tea leaves, and sipped in silence. Neither host nor hostess, nor the honored guest exchanges dialogue.

Far more than the drinking of tea occurs. *Cha-No-Yu* has to do with the roots of existence. "It is the art of cultivating the psychosphere, or the inner field of consciousness." It is the "aestheticism of primitive simplicity," states Suzuki.[101] All the artifical wrappings of human devising are swept away. Its purpose is to intensify an intuitive grasp of reality. All of its components unite in assisting the participants to become one with the simple state of things, without doctrines interrupting their immediate awareness of their oneness with nature.

For Suzuki, four character-building motifs are associated with the art of drinking tea: *harmony, reverence, purity*, and *tranquility*. All are requisite for a fulfilled existence, and without them, we are less than human, less than nature has instilled within us the capacity to become. Here is a version of the spirituality of creation, second to none.

In North America, the sun dance incorporates many facets of nature, rendering it too as a communion service, uniting participants with themselves and nature and the transcendent mystery of the *Wakan Tanka*. From the cottonwood tree that is selected with care; to its implacement in a socket of the earth, surrounded with buffalo fat; to the four colors posted to the tree, representing the four quarters of the earth; to the eagle claw used to tear open human flesh, the eagle representing the eye of God; to the sweat-bath of purity required of the dancers, who dance only in response to a vision, dream, or vow; to the suffering that occurs that unites them all; and to the miracles of healing that erupt beneath the tree, the spirituality of the earth is recognized and hallowed. Theirs is a reverence for life unequalled anywhere. With a willingness to pay the cost.

Christianity's own tree, the cross, is a symbol of nature as well, and so is the body of Christ. "For as often as you eat this bread and drink this cup, you proclaim the Lord's death until he comes." The Reformer John Calvin extolled the Lord's Supper, not merely because

---

[101] Ibid., p. 271.

of its saving powers, but because of its nurturing capacity to unite humanity with the true bread of life.

Along a similar but different line is a parable that Chuang Tsu tells in his *Inner Chapters.* One finds it in Chapter Four, under "Human Affairs." It is the story of the hunchback named Shu. Terribly disfigured, he was exempt from military conscription and the corvee that built public projects. Instead, he earned his livelihood by sewing, taking in laundry, and sifting and winnowing grain. When the government gave grain to the sick, he received three measures and several bundles of firewood. If a man so disfigured can take care of himself, observes Chuang Tsu, then shouldn't a man of "strange behavior," or one who adopts Shu's philosophy, come to the end of his natural life much easier? Chuang Tsu knew what it meant to "let go" and flow with the mystery of life, true to one's nature. His parable is not far from Jesus's words of Matthew 5:3: "Blessed are the poor in spirit, for theirs is the kingdom of God." It is the wisdom that lies at the heart of the Buddha's self-emptying and André's principle of "poverty" before God.

Perhaps the most demanding vision of the spirituality of the earth, is that expressed in the *Bhagavad-Gita*, in Krishna's speech to Arjuna. The latter is hesistant to take up his dharma, his duty as a warrior, and lead his people forward. So the Godhead descends in the form of Krishna and counsels Arjuna on the eve of the battle. It is one of the most powerful insights that reflects the conviction that we have come from a universe whose pulsations never dim in the unending mystery of life. According to Krishna: there has never been a time when the Godhead did not exist, nor in the future will anyone cease to be. A true yogi observes the Godhead in all beings, and sees every being in the Godhead. Indeed, the self-realized man sees the Godhead everywhere. And for anyone who sees the Godhead everywhere and sees everything in the Godhead, that person can never cease to exist.

The rarefied teachings of Hinduism may seem esoteric to some, but the truth of humanity's linkage with nature and all that transcends the mystery of being is avowed in the *Bhagavad-Gita*. Life is a journey even for Arjuna, a battle which he cannot avoid. The plain of life stretches before him. Conflict is inevitable. There is a dark side to Being. But life and death are ultimately one, part of the same mystery. For each there is a time under heaven. Arjuna's challenge is to take heart and entrust his soul to the God of Being. In Him, he cannot go wrong. And so Arjuna lurches forward as the chariot thunders into battle. "It is a good day to die!" cried the brave warriors.

From Judaism comes a different story, but at its heart lies the Lakota truth: "All over the earth the faces of living things are all alike." It is a story from Martin Buber's *Tales of the Hasidim*. It is founded on the mystery of God's omnipresence and *hesed* love, on his loyalty to the house of Israel. It is entitled, "If Not Higher?" It underscores the love of a Jewish congregation for its rabbi. They were confident he knew of a rendezvous spot for meeting God. So one Yom Kippur, during the rabbi's absence from the synagogue, they commissioned one of their own to follow the rabbi. To the follower's surprise, the rabbi's path led to the home of an invalid woman. There the rabbi disrobed, put on a peasant's smock, fed and cared for the old woman, then redonned his vestments to return to the synagogue. The appointed "spy" hurried ahead of the rabbi. "Did he ascend to heaven?" the congregation asked. To which the man replied, "If not higher?"

Islam is often perceived as a harsh religion, but in the *Hadith* literature of al-Bukhari one stumbles upon this gem: "A Bedouin came to the Prophet and said, 'Do you kiss children? We never do.' And the Prophet said, 'What shall I do to give back to you the mercy God has taken from your heart?'"[102] Bukhari preserves a story, even about a dog. A traveler once found himself thirsty and coming upon a well, climbed inside for a drink. Struggling back out he discovered a dog, also at thirst. Its tongue was hanging out and the dog was licking the earth. So he redescended the well, took off his shoe, filled it with water, and with the shoe clinched in his teeth, reclimbed the well and gave the dog to drink. Is there a reward for such pity? the Prophet was asked. "Yes. There is a reward on every living creature."[103]

In his *A Sand County Almanac*, Aldo Leopold relives a scene from his boyhood days. It marked the occasion that he became a man, awakened to the value of every living thing. He and other companions were on a rimrock, overlooking a bend in the river. Perceiving what they thought to be a deer, they watched as the doe swam the current. But once ashore, they realized the animal was a wolf. Soon she was joined by her pack of pups. At once, the onlookers began firing with their rifles, to rid the rimrock country of the wolves. They managed to

---

[102] See John A. Williams, *Islam* (New York: Geroge Braziller, 1962), p. 83.
[103] Ibid., p. 85.

fell the wolf and then clamored down the rock to admire their kill. Leopold tells the rest:

> We reached the old wolf in time to watch a fierce green fire dying in her eyes. I realized then, and have known ever since, that there was something new to me in those eyes--something known only to her and to the mountain. I was young then, and full of trigger-itch; I thought that because fewer wolves meant more deer, that no wolves would mean hunters' paradise. But after seeing the green fire die, I sensed that neither the wolf nor the mountain agreed with such a view.[104]

There is no substitute for reverence for life. It has the potential to deepen our humanity and bind us together, as well as to the mystery of Being itself.

That night at Gethsemane, Jesus was forced to make a decision that changed the course of history. It is possible that he and his followers could have slipped away, descended unnoticed the road to Jericho, and holed up in Qumran until passions faded in Jerusalem. Then they could have returned to Galilee, unscathed.

But Jesus was Jesus and he had come to Jerusalem in obedience to a voice he could not deny. "Father, if it is possible, let this cup pass from me. Nonetheless, not my will but yours be done." He elected to stay and complete his journey. "Into your hands I commend my spirit."

If we ourselves are to fulfill our existence, we too have to be obedient to the voice of Being as we are graced to hear it. That Voice speaks many languages, I am certain. Older dogmas may cease to reach us, no longer feed us, no longer lead us. But our oneness with the universe cannot be denied. Nor can the silent voice of Being. Listen within and you will feel it. Sit by a stream and you will hear it. Talk to a friend and you will meet it. Empty yourself and it will enter.

---

[104] Aldo Leopold, *A Sand County Almanac* (New York: Oxford University Press, 1966), p. 130.

Chapter 29

The Son of Galilee

In the early 1900s, Albert Schweitzer published a book whose shadow still falls across the entire century. It was entitled *The Quest of the Historical Jesus.* In it he traced the views of the past two centuries' best scholarly minds concerning the identity of Jesus. From the earlier suppressed questions of Hermann Reimarus (1694-1768), who warned that one must distinguish between the teachings of Jesus versus the teachings of his disciples, to the more confident conclusions of William Wrede (1859-1906), who argued that Mark's picture of Jesus is far more theological than it is hisitorical, the self-consciousness of the historical Jesus was pursued. Schweitzer's own conclusions were mystical and liberal. Jesus thought he could hasten the Kingdom's arrival by actions of his own. But his plan failed. He was arrested and tried, crucified and buried, and his disciples fled. But Schweitzer was hooked. He had come to love Jesus, and, abandoning his promising career as a New Testament scholar, he retrained as a physician and sailed to Africa to heal that continent's lame and ill. Schweitzer's closing words of his *Quest* now read like scripture:

> He comes to us as One unknown, without a name, as of old,
> by the lake-side, He came to those men who knew Him not.
> He speaks to us the same word: "Follow thou me!" and sets
> us to the tasks which He has to fulfil for our time. He
> commands. And to those who obey Him, whether they be
> wise or simple, He will reveal Himself in the toils, the
> conflicts, the sufferings which they shall pass through in His

fellowship, and, as an ineffable mystery, they shall learn in their own experience Who He is.[105]

Since Schweitzer, two additional quests have swept through the scholarly halls of New Testament studies. Rudolf Bultmann led one, concluding that we can never know anything positively about the identity, or self-consciousness, of the historical Jesus of Nazareth. All we have are the writings of the evangelists, who were already wed to their communities' views. At best, we must settle for the *form* and *setting* of Jesus' sayings, combined with legends and the Passion story of his last week in Jerusalem. His theory, labeled "form criticism," is still used and taught at all major seminaries. Yet even for Bultmann Jesus remains the Son of God and Savior of the world. For Jesus's own self-awareness of God and God's radical call to faith "here and now," in spite of anxiety, ambiguity, and finitude, serve to awaken human consciousness, making the choice for a more authentic life possible.

The third quest is still under way, still in debate. Among its many participants, two in particular attract attention: Burton Mack and John Dominic Crossan. The first has devoted his study to Jesus' sayings, to the famous lost Gospel of Q, a document that underlies much of Matthew and Luke's account of Jesus' speech. Q is an abbreviation for the German word *Quelle*, wich means "source." It has to do with the source containing Jesus' teachings. Mack believes that Q existed in written form and underwent three editions. The first contained the original sayings of Jesus and alone witnesses to the true Jesus of history. The second and third editions enlarged upon Jesus' words. They shifted the emphasis of his aphoristic maxims and imperatives, which had to do with life and God, to an emphasis on the *man* himself, and to the growing myth that was accruing in the Jesus communities, especially outside Galilee. But the need for Q ceased and the document itself dropped out of existence, once the gospels were written and the mythic elements were included in Matthew and Luke. Mack's work has been a prodigious attempt to capture afresh the real Jesus, the historical Jesus, the Jesus of Nazareth himself.

---

[105] Albert Schweitzer, *The Quest of the Historical Jesus* (New York: Macmillan, Co., 1964), p. 403.

Crossan's work is entitled *The Essential Jesus*. His program is also aimed at uncovering the real Jesus, or the essential Jesus, if possible. But for Crossan, Jesus is less of a sage (as he is for Mack) and more of a revolutionary, who pursued both a religious and a social program in the Lower Galilee, and paid for it with his life. Crossan makes a distinction between *apocalyptic eschatology* and *sapiential eschatology*. The former has to do with faithful souls awaiting on God to act in order to negate life's exploitative forces; the latter has to do with humans acting on their own to end life's oppressive powers. Jesus chose the way of the latter. For Crossan, Jesus' parables and aphorisms clearly attest to a radical egalitarianism, in which the Kingdom of God is accessible for anyone of courage to enact in his or her time.

By way of addendum, Mack depicts a Jesus who was in debt to the epic dimensions of his Jewish past, as well as his love of nature, in which he saw the providential hand of the Father. All else is *Vorstellung*, which has now been taken up in doctrines and dogmas. My own journey and "divine gift," the gift of doubt, lure me in Mack's direction. Without oversimplifying the problem, much in the story of the Son of Galilee conforms to Mack's depiction. The gospels portray a Jesus who clearly sensed an affinity with nature, who perceived its spirituality, and opened himself to the mystery and will of its Creator. "You are the light of the world, the salt of the earth." "Look at the birds of the air; they neither sow nor reap nor gather into barns, and yet your heavenly Father feeds them.... Consider the lilies of the field, how they grow;... yet I tell you, even Solomon in all his glory was not clothed like one of these." "Love your enemies and pray for those who persecute you, so that you may be children of your Father in heaven, for he makes his sun rise on the evil and on the good, and sends rain on the righteous and unrighteous." "Our Father, which art in heaven, hallowed be thy name. Thy kingdom come, thy will be done, on earth as it is in heaven." All of the qualities of reverence for life, trust in its goodness, and relatedness with all fellow humans, are endorsed here.

Although I find Crossan's and Mack's views intriguing, many Christians do not. Traditional Christianity remains surprisingly resilient, reluctant to accept any form of the denial of Christ's "divine mystery." His transcendent otherness is simply non-negotiable; nor can his universal transparency as the unique symbol of transcendence and humanity be compromised.

A metaphysical "God-man" seems strangely out of place in today's world. Yet, a metaphorical "God-man" might just be what the world needs. One who is fully human, yet fully an embodiment of the Mystery of the universe, its wonder and beauty, intrinsic goodness and possibilities. Indeed, Christianty's claim is that Christ is precisely that man.

From a metaphorical perspective, the incarnation, the virgin birth, and the resurrection all testify to a profound longing and profound truth.

Take the matter of the incarnation. It is not unique to Christianity. The present-day Dalai Lama is no one less than the 14th reincarnation of the spirit of the Compassionate Buddha himself. In Hinduism, Rama, Krishna, and the Buddha are all considered *avatars*, descents, incarnations, of Brahman. So also the pharaohs were incarnations of the god Re. In Christianity the belief is founded on John 1:1-4, 14.

> In the beginning was the Word (logos), and the Word was with
> God, and the Word was God. He was in the beginning with
> God. All things came into being through him, and without
> him not one thing came into being. What has come into
> being in him was life, and the life was the light of all people
> And the Word became flesh and lived among us.

At its heart, this Johannine interpretation of the Son of Galilee declares that in his life humanity was offered a principle of intelligibilty that has the power to make intelligible all the other moments of human existence. It means that "life" and "light," being and meaning, are grounded in an Infinite Reality that is both knowable and immanent, however transcendent as well. For the Johannine community, the life of Christ made that reality so transparent, that it brought joy and hope, meaning and purpose, to all who could see it.

We too are bounded by the parameters of being and meaning, "life" and "light," nature and transcendence. What the incarnation declares is that the Mystery that engenders life is the same Mystery that illumines its purpose. Such a Mystery is already immanent in the universe, if we but had the eyes to see it. Its quest is what science and religion are both about.

For Native Americans, it is the cycles of time, the seasonal changes, the powers of nature, and the spiritual forces that reverberate through them that bond together to sanctify life, rendering all of its entities holy. The *tunkashila* within and behind the universe, the *nagi* that nudges the soul, the sacred *Wakan Tanka* are all manifestations of a logos become flesh. All are noetic witnesses to the reality of a Creator.

The virgin birth also bespeaks of this quest. It witnesses with awe to a wonder that lies at the soul of the miracle of life. On Christmas Eve it takes on a heightened quality, as humanity stares with the shepherds of old into that tiny face of the babe, wrapped in swaddling clothes, lying in a Bethlehem manger. The story evokes powerful feelings of self-examination as well, because it brings us face to face with a disturbing emptiness within. It releases deeply repressed yearnings for wholeness again, of longings for that alone which can regenerate peace, goodness, hope, and love. Above all, it stirs us to ponder the possibility of a higher order, that perhaps we truly belong to an Infinite Otherness, that we are part of a kingdom whose time and boundaries both overlap and transcend our own, providing our wisest and happiest path to follow. The true *tathata*.

As for the resurrection, its universal truth is equally unmistakable. Evil was never meant to have the last word, nor does it have to have the last word. There is an intrinsic goodness to life, to nature, to beingness, to the Mystery. To commit our lives and hopes into its hands is to transcend naysaying, hate, prejudice, fear, and suffering. But it always comes at a price, a high cost, requiring an act of incredible courage and faith in the holy Giver of life, whether that Giver is nature, the *Wakan Tanka*, the Buddha essence, or God.

Jesus died at a time when Hellenistic religion was at its lowest, or most frenzied, ebb and mystery cults swept the ancient world. From the worship of Isis in Egypt and North Africa to the cult of Demeter and Cybele in Asia Minor and Rome, gods and goddesses were passionately sought after to reinvigorate one's world. The accounts of blood-drawings and lashings, castrations and scourgings that accompanied the orgies associated with Cybele may still be read. All one has to do is turn to Lucian's famous work: *De Syria Dea.* But gone was the voice of a Plato or Aristotle; gone were the plays in honor of Dionysus. Mankind was athirst for a new wine to slake its throat. Jesus of Nazareth became that new wine. He represented a humbler Dionysus, without the blood-letting of a Cybele; he symbolized a new promise for immortality, a new gateway to hope and peace. Thus his life and teachings became a logos, a new enlightenment become flesh, the new Apollo of illumination and order.

The centuries press on. But Jesus' openness to God can never be repressed, nor his poverty before the Infinite. He never pretended to know what was beyond his capacity to know. "Blessed are the poor in spirit, for theirs is the kingdom of heaven." "Suffer the little children to come unto me, for of such is the kingdom of heaven."

For a modern era, the Son of Galilee lived just once, *einmal und nicht mehr*. But in Christian hearts, he lives on. He still speaks from his cross: "Father, into your hands I commend my spirit." And his sensitivity toward all who suffer, his compassion for all who mourn, and his kindness toward others, survives and survives and survives. In that he is still the Savior, who manifests the mystery of Being. A brother who shows the way. The Son of Galilee. The Son of God. The manifestation of the mystery of our human condition.

Chapter 30
Pain, Evil, and Suffering

"Pain shatters the illusion that all is well," that our own strength is "sufficient," wrote C.S. Lewis (1898-1963).[106] Why have I saved this chapter to the last? For many human beings, pain is the greatest mystery of our humanness, as well as its gravest threat. Nonetheless, however we come at pain, we never escape the realm of nature and spirit. Pain, evil, and suffering make explicit what being human is all about. They are functions of our human essence, at both its physiological and psychological level. To understand this is to be spared the anxiety of asking either God or nature why suffering has to exist.

At the natural, biological, and physiological level, pain is inevitable. So too is suffering. Pain belongs to the nature of *athamah*, or dust. No arcane theories are required to understand that without central nervous systems *Homo sapiens sapiens* could not have evolved. A "painful" reaction to negative stimuli is nature's way of protecting its progeny, not harming them. The hand that is suddenly withdrawn from the burning fire survives to hurl a spear, skin a hide, caress a mate, or tousle a child's hair.

At the natural level, pain and suffering can hone the body, strengthen its muscles, grip, and endurance, and grace the form of the self-disciplined. It can become a noble instrument for shaping one's own inner character. It can equally be devastating and destructive, causing one to turn against God and life, and even long for Brother Death!

---

[106] See C.S. Lewis, *The Problem of Pain* (London: Geoffrey Bles, 1940).

The same holds true for the sphere of *ru'ah*, the realm of self-consciousness and freedom. Our awareness of moral pain and moral sorrow grows directly out of our capacity to put our choices and conduct to the question. No theologies of retribution and atonement are necessary to understand that human thought and action produce inordinate amounts of suffering and evil, both for ourselves and others. Frequently the only correctives are self-imposed forms of "suffering," or renunciation, such as self-denial, self-sacrifice, and self-discipline.

Evil is another matter. Most of us would define evil as any form of suffering that is willed upon another so as to diminish that person. We might extend the definition to include harm to the environment and the earth's irreplacable species as well. To put ourselves to the test, or to test ourselves as a people, however, is not an evil. All the warriors, athletes, saints, sages, and martrys of old did as much and would extol our own era to experience the cleansing power of renunciation. Evil, however, is the result of suffering that grows out of disrespect for others, or that is motivated by greed, selfishiness, envy, ignorance, and spite. Such suffering avails no ultimate good.

If evil had a dawn, I suppose it occurred the first time a member of *Homo erectus* knowingly smiled to himself, having caused pain for another being. Pain inflicted or endured in the process of survival and self-defense is one thing; even levels of elation in battle and the hunt are acceptable. But deliberatley inflicting pain on another is something else. Even the old doctrine of "an eye for an eye and a tooth for a tooth" is founded on the principle of respect. To harm anyone is a grave matter and requires accountability, along with restraint on the part of those who administer justice.

The Buddha was 35 when he experienced enlightenment, or woke up and saw things as they are. He devoted the remaining 45 years of his life to fashioning a "path" that would minimize moral sorrow and eliminate as much unnecessary pain as possible. It was his way of bringing his own life into harmony with his *athamah* and *ru'ah*.

Without oversimplifying the Buddha's discovery, central to his thought is the realization that a self-centered consciousness is detrimental to its own good. A self-consciousness that can never transcend its own ego constantly gets in the way of its unity with other beings as well as the mystery of the universe. A self that is perpetually engaged in craving generates unending conflict, jealousy, bitterness, and unhappiness. One must simply renounce such a self and empty it of its delusions and desires. Thus the Buddha embraced a form of self-suffering, of renunciation, in order to eliminate world suffering.

To achieve this the Buddha recommended an Eightfold Path, in which he encouraged: 1) accurate perceptions, or seeing things as they are, 2) accurate thinking, free of diversion and digression, 3) careful speech, avoiding gossip and deceit, 4) appropriate action, suited to the occasion, 5) an appropriate career for earning one's livelihood, 6) precise effort, 7) right recollection, and 8) earnest concentration.

His *Dhammapada* is filled with admonitions in which he urges his followers to move beyond the self, if not master the self, in order to master suffering and, thus, move beyond pain.

> Hatreds do not cease in this world by hatred, but by not hating.
> Do not look at the faults of others, or what others have done or not done; observe what you yourself have done and have not done.
> It is better to live one day ethically and reflectively than to live a hundred years immoral and unrestrained.
> One who uses goodness to cover the evil he has done lights up the world like an unclouded moon.
> Not insulting, not injuring, self-discipline, moderation in consumption, solitude, exertion in mental concentration--this is the teaching of the Buddhas.[107]

For C. S. Lewis, pain, evil, and suffering are facets of a larger order that God wills. They are components of a "tribulational system" that recognizes that all choices lead to consequences for which we are accountable.

Lewis finds no difficulty is squaring such a "tribulational system" with either the goodness or wisdom of God. God is intrinsically good and wise. Since God is the highest good, choices for God inevitably result in pain, as humanity rises above desires and ends that thwart its own development. "Unless a grain of wheat fall into the earth and die, it cannot bear fruit" (John 12:24,KJV). "In the world you have tribulation," said Jesus, "but be of good cheer, for I have overcome the world" (John 16:33). Both of these sayings capture the essence of

---

[107] See Thomas Cleary's *Dhammapada: The Sayings of the Buddha* (New York: Bantam Books, 1995), pp. 8, 21, 40, 60, and 64 respectively.

spirituality in its universal form: that there is something larger than the self for which we live that alone bestows life's highest satisfaction.

In this respect, Lewis and the Buddha share a common vision of the highest good. The Lakota concept of bravery and endurance, along with the Stoic's drive for self-mastery draw from the same well. Concludes Lewis: "The full acting out of the self's surrender to God ... demands pain." Or as the Buddha surmised: "The life of mortals is hard."[108]

Because pain, evil, and suffering belong to the order of nature and transcendence, they can be explained along humanistic lines as well. No recourse to God is necessary. For the humanist, good and evil lie totally within the human domain. As Kai Nielsen, a contemporary Canadian philosopher, contends, we alone are responsible for discovering those "panhuman" ideals, values, and interests that advance humanity.[109] Our capacity for self-consciousness and reflection, along with our awareness of our common social interdependence, are sufficient resources for compelling us to eliminate as much pain as possible. No one can do it for us. Postponing it until the afterlife is both cowardly and an affront to a modern era. We must do it for ourselves, or it will never become a reality.

From a scientific perspective, pain is an inescapable facet of evolution. The survival of the fittest, the adaptation of species, and the advancement of mankind have all come about through the earth's species coping with challenge and the phenomenon of pain. Without it, creation, development, self-realization, and fulfillment are impossible.

From a religious perspective, pain, evil, and suffering constitute the ultimate mystery. Not all pain is redemptive. Not all evil results in a higher good. Much human suffering, though understandable, can rarely, if ever, be justified. It is a product of our ignorance, transcendence, and of a freedom to make choices that can create woe for millions worldwide. When it cannot be justified, what is humanity to do? Fault God? Fault nature? Or accept it and go on? Ultimately, Job himself chose the latter. His answer still endures. After losing his children, property, and wealth, his wife said to him:

---

[108] Ibid., p. 63.
[109] See Nielsen's *Marx and Morality, New Essays in Ethics and Public Policy, In Defense of Atheism* and other works.

"Why don't you curse God and die?" "No, no!" he replied. "Shall we receive the good from the hand of God, and not receive the bad? Though God slay me, yet will I trust him" (Job 2:10; 13:15). It was Job's way of affirming the mystery of existence, as we all must do, in spite of finitude, anxiety, despair, and the threat of nonbeing.

In the final analysis, as all the wise have known, the mystery of life forces us to choose between one of two ends: to light a lamp, or curse the darkness. All other choices fade in comparison.

"You are the light of the world," said Jesus. "Good people shine from afar, like the Snowy Mountains," said the Buddha.

This side of eternity, there are no other lights, no other shiny mountains, save yours and mine. Both Teachers understood the challenge of this truth; neither flinched before it; each lived it to the end. And they have transmitted it to us, in humility and boldness, for our own challenge and joy, hope and peace.

Epilogue

The old farm roads have all been paved along the ridges. Deep in the weeds, dusty lanes and cattle paths trail off into the bramble. From the road's shadows, one can see an occasional barn, an abandoned tenant shack, and rotting fence posts. They molder, dank and canted, between the stands of pine and oakwoods. One passes them so quickly where they hover in fallow fields, waist-high in broomsedge and thicket. They form a soft mosaic of sodden boards, rusting tin roofs, faded red shingles, and greenish-gray lichen.

In the winter, patches of light fog drift through the hardwoods and settle in gray furrows along the creekbanks. Here tips of pine stand silhouetted against the fog, while distant ridges dim along the horizon.

Once the sun rises, the fog dissipates, leaving the weeds and tall grass wet with dew, and heralds a clean, bright morning.

It is such a morning, as I pull my car on to the shoulder of the road, bring it to a stop, and cut off the engine.

I look out across the mist, the fields, the trees, the bottom. I step out of my car and listen to the silence. The sun is rising, but the mist is still heavy. Slowly the mist begins to glow a bright yellow. The fog clears, and I am standing in the rays of the morning sun. The mist has dissipated, but its presence has moved within. The rays of the sun feel soft and warm; its orange center has become a shimmering glare.

It is a new day, and I will soon be at work, "counting coup" on students at the college where I teach. But just now, I am a son of the morning sky, part of the earth's being, as I raise my hand to my brow to count the ridges along the horizon.

Suddenly, to my right, a field of young pines comes alive.   A frightened covey of quail explodes into the air. They sail past me, scattering into the hardwoods behind the car. Then, I spot the fox. His nose is black, his flanks gray, his throat and tail a rusty red. He hops out into the field of broomsedge, which is in front of both of us, and suddenly stops. He turns his face toward me, his gray body in profile. I can see his nose, his beady eyes. He observes me carefully, sniffs the air, then lopes on across the field into a stand of hardwoods.   He disappears into its vines and brush.

Hey, hey! brother fox! May the four winds bless you! May *tunkashila* guard and keep you!   May he make the light of his countenance to shine upon you and keep your going out and your coming in from this time forth and ever more. Sister quail. Brother bobwhite. Fear not. It is a good day to fly, to hide, to feed, to preen, as you peck your way along your Mother Earth.

It is late. But the sun is warm. And it fills me with its winter radiance. But it is time to break off. Time to move on. Time to "count coup" on my students. Time to invade their thoughts and hearts with the mystery of Being. In all its myriad forms.

Thank you, Father Sky. Thank you, Mother Earth, for this moment together.

It is I. Just one of your many sons, who greets you.

And to You, most holy and silent One within. The Mystery of Being. Fill me with the joy and gratitude of Your Presence all the days of my life.

An Epilegomenon for Further Reflections

In the mind of many Christians, there has been in our time a profound and powerful movement to repaganize the Faith. Certainly, Christian professors involved in teaching college courses in philosophy of religion, science and religion, world religions, Native American studies, and contemporary spirituality are fully aware of this development. Generally, they attempt to be very descrete in their handling of fringe movements that border on the satanic and the occult, but they do not dismiss these as subjects unworthy of study. Being open to a scientific exploration of the universe, however, and to the historical religious traditions of other peoples is a different matter. It is essential to academia.

Engagement at intercultural levels can be highly rewarding and illuminating. At the same time, it requires a willingness to reexamine ones own belief system with humility and integrity. When this occurs, a host of possibilities and issues surface. In all candor, many of these issues are challenging, and no pat answers do justice to their complexity. I would summarize the primary issues as: 1) that God, in the Judeo-Christian-Moslem sense, is a Western concept and that other concepts of "God" are also viable; 2) that the universe, for all of its mystery, is sufficiently explicable in terms of its own phenomena; 3) that making peace with this "fact" and bringing one's life into harmony with the universe is an important prerequisite for human happiness; and 4) that any one of a plethora of spiritual ways can promote the attainment of inner peace, although some of these ways are fraught with obstacles and limitations for a secular age.

I can't image how anyone can deny the power of this *engagement's* appeal. I have struggled with it all my teaching life. As

Son of the Morning Sky attests, I am a lover of science and nature, as well as humbled by the reality of the Infinite. I welcome the viewpoint of the scientists, the biologists, and naturalists. And as an outdoorsman, I have always been drawn to the voice of God in the sough of the wind in the forest and in the gurgling whisper of the trickling brook.

The truth is, both science and religion are under attack today. There are not only hordes of contemporary despisers of religion, but there are legions who fear science's presuppostions and findings and who attempt to shield themselves and their children from its premises and truths. Both voices, however, are necessary. One does not have to be a fanatic to be religious. At the same time, one can endorse the most challenging precepts of science, savor the silence of nature and its healing powers, and remain a lover of the Infinite. Equally, one does not have to abandon one's religious heritage to avoid appearing unappreciative of other traditions. Once can applaud the profoundest depths of truth that persons of other persuasions cherish, while remaining faithful to the vision of the Sacred that one's own religion espouses.

Is it illusory to believe that one can have it both ways? That one can embrace the full measure of the tenets of science, while remaining humble and religiously open, if not even committed to a Christian or Buddhist way? The former, at least, would have to include the beliefs: 1) that God exists, 2) that the universe, the Big Bang, and evolution are facets of God's will, 3) that God is knowable, 4) that since the dawn of human consciousness, God has been active, drawing humanity toward a growing awareness of the divine, and 5) that, for Christians, the Christ of the Gospels remains the supreme witness to and embodiment of the reality, mystery, and grace of God. Without oversimplying it, the Buddhist way would substitute the "Buddha essence" for God and the Buddha for the Christ, as the most transparent form of that essence.

Finally, spiritual movements in our time (such as the New Age movement), have often been panned as evil by many well-meaning Christian theologians. I believe they are wrong to do so. Why? Because these movements represent a variety of realities and yearnings that beg to be heard, not dismissed. What are these?

First, that in light of our knowledge of how religions and various cultures have evolved and developed, a dialogue and an openness toward one another's heritage is wiser than insisting on an exclusivist claim. The simple truth is that many people find the insights of the Buddha, Black Elk and others helpful, and their acknowledgement of such is not meant to detract in any way from their commitment to Christ, or from their admiration of Jesus.

Second, that today's spiritually hungry people have been educated in a secular era, in which the parameters of science are taken to be "true," or at least are respected as the best valid working hypotheses we have. Thus, as a group, they are unwilling to endorse doctrines that ignore or dismiss scientific findings. For example, is there life after death? Some Westerners have reexamined the Hindu principle of reincarnantion and have found it appealing, but many others are content to accept the mystery of the genetic code as bearer of any significant past or future continuance and leave to God the hope of any future existence.

Third, that concrete individual experiences, especially those set in the orders of Nature, are as rich in meaning and value as some Scriptural texts, laden with prescientific presuppositions. For example, many Native American shamans value a rich materialistic surrounding of objects that carry high symbolic meaning. Rocks and precious stones, the colors of the rainbow, plants and various aromatic branches, drums, vision pits, dances, the powwow, ritual steam baths, sage and tobacco smoke, to name but a few, are all endowed with special value. All are tangible, visible realities. They serve in a sacramental capacity, helping the searcher to see and feel and smell and touch something that is invisible and intangible, but nonetheless longed for and hallowed. The other phenomenon is nature itself, the silence and beauty of the created order. Retreating to it can bring tremendous peace and inner serenity. There one walks in the cool of the garden, surrounded by its mists and forests, one's soul strangely open to the voice of Being, to the entire sweep of the cosmos and its Mystery.

Finally, humanity today yearns for meaning and purposefulness, just as any previous era has done. But it must be a meaning compatible with our general knowledge of the world, its vulnerability, finitude, and temporariness. To long for more stretches one's credulity. For the most part, modern humanity is hesitant to sacrifice its intelligence for a faith system that our scientific knowledge of the universe cannot sustain. In that regard, *humility before the Infinite* may be the only dogma that a contemporary spirituality can endorse with certitude in our time. Anything more than that begs the question. Yet anything less denies the acknowledged *ru'ah* in all living things.

As Job captured the challenge in his time:

> But ask the animals, and they will teach you;
> the birds of the air, and they will tell you;
> ask the plants of the earth, and they will delcare to you;
> and the fish of the sea will declare to you.
> Who among these does not know that the hand of the Lord has done this?
> In his hand is the life of every living thing
> and the breath of every human being (Job 12:7-10).

POEMS OF THE KNOBS

BY

THE AUTHOR

Down From The Knobs Each Winter He Came

Down from the Knobs each winter he came
Wrapped in scarves and swollen veins.
Gaunt and wrinkled and bent in frame
He'd sit with his back to the window.

With cap on knee, his hair growing thin,
He'd creak the rungs of the kitchen chair
And gaze at the cookstove's ironware
And tall tea kettle that whistled there.

"Kate," he'd commence, as he rubbed his chin,
Warming his knuckles and sallow skin,
"You know I'm restless and given to roam.
I know," he'd look up, "God made the Knobs,

"The spring and the summer and golden cobs,
The sourwood blossom and honeycomb,
The corn and the hay and the orchard tree,
And, best of all, made you and me.

"But, Kate, the thing that puzzles me still,
When I tromp the frozen mud and sod,
Or plant potatoes come spring in a hill,
Is who, just who, Miz Kate, made God?"

Aunt Bess

He came to the kitchen door that night
While fryers sizzled on the stove.
"Any chores I can do, Miz White?
Afore I head up cove?"

      He'd already worked since light of day,
      Suckering tobacco, mowing hay,
      Stitching sacs for the wheat and barley
      harvest.

He clutched the brim of his crumpled hat.
The tobacco gum on his hands gleamed black,
His fingers red with the Knob's clay soil,
His moist shirt rank with sweat and toil.

She knew he still had paths to climb
Up past rocks and briar vines,
Eight mouths to feed and a wife in need,
Their hearth, a red dirt floor.

And but for a shank of streaked meat
She had given the man last week
It worried her what the ten would eat
Save for cornmeal cores.

"Nubby, if you would slop the hogs--
The pails are by the door."
And while he set about his chore
She quickly set about hers.

A platter of chicken she divided in half
With a pile of biscuits in a napkin wrapped
Along with a jar and a cake of butter.

"Here," she pushed them in his hands,
As he came up from the sty.
"Stop by the springhouse on your way.
Take some cream to Sally Mae.

"No need to thank Jim or me,"
She brushed him off with a smile.
He left by the gate and, tipping his hat,
Hurried toward the springhouse stile.

She watched him go, then turned about
And stared at the stove for awhile,
Then wrang her hands in her apron cloth
And peered out the screen once more.

Hawks

Two hawks soared high
Climbing drafts in clear cold sky
Each circled the other, looped and dived,
Hawk crying to hawk,
Their black and white wing marks clearly visible.

Their aerobatics or romantics satisfied
They circled higher
And disappeared behind peaks of pine
Beyond a fallow rise of sumac in briar.

Pretty Girl of the Knobs

Pretty girl of the Knobs
In your flour sack dress
Milk pail in hand
And shawl about your breasts.

Oh, where are you bound
With your smile wide and free
Your pigtail long
And cheeks blushing?

I run to keep up,
Past the pens, past the hogs,
I run to keep up,
Pretty girl of the Knobs.

You pause by the barn,
I see him within.
Your eyes glance at me
And then back to him.

Oh, where are you bound
Pretty girl of the Knobs
With your smile wide and free
And cheeks blushing?

Oh, where are you bound
In your flour sack dress
With your pigtail down
And your shawl off your breasts?

That Drought May Pass

The sweltering heat and torpid air
Have seared the land and left it bare.

With pastures dry, turned crisp and brown,
The July sun hath scorched the ground.

Nor fields yield crops nor grain yield blade
Nor cattle graze by cool of shade.

Nor creeks run free nor clouds bring rain
No dews to quench the lost quail's plaint.

And farmers walk the crackling grass
And pray that soon the drought may pass.

Big John Coleman

And after the rhetoric, what then?
Words cannot resuscitate the dead.
I will watch the inked-in name cards fade.
And when I see your face, remote and drawn,
I'll understand the loss, that he is gone.

Thor

I have seen Thor
Walking at night
Carrying his bulky lanterns.

There he is now
Swinging them up
Behind the clouds.

Thou hast grown old
Legendary god.
How thy lamps
Tremble in thy hands!

Even the sound
Of thy passing
Rumbles, feebly.

It is night
And lightning flashes softly
Outlining clouds high above the Knobs.

For Whom the Heart Doth Pine

Now you have come to your rocker
To lull away the pain
To say farewell to the homeplace
You will never indwell again.

I pass by ever so quietly
In the mirror your profile asway
You came in the year he retired
And widowed will move away.

For thirty-three years you both lived here
In memory, content, and at peace
And now we pack your china
Piece by fragile piece.

And never send to know
For whom the heart doth pine
For fifty-eight years you loved him
Whom sod and grave confine.

So rock, dear Mother, rock
And lull away your pain
And bid farewell to the homeplace
You will never indwell again.

Sun Rise

Calm, cold, pale, clear morning sky
Etched by windbreaks of pine and cedar
We wake to enter your brisk estate
Grateful for night and dawn.

Hide Me In The Chinquapins

Hide me in the chinquapins
Where the rocks are broad and flat
And wild, thick ripe strawberries
Are luscious, sweet, and fat.

O Trixie, Trixie,
I found your chain one day
High upon the chinquapin hill
Where Panther led you away.

The fire crackles on the hearth
Chair rungs softly cry,
O Trixie, Trixie, old gal
Where do you lie?

Where did Panther take you
When he unlatched your chain
And gently held the pistol
Against your tired brain?

O Uncle Clark and Woody,
The moon tonight is bright
And you and I are somewhere
Still tramping through the night.

Hide me in the chinquapins
Where the rocks are broad and flat
Where wild, thick ripe strawberries
Are luscious, sweet, and fat.

And sing for me, Granny
O please, for me Granny sing.
For I am old and wiser now
And wear a wedding ring.

At Dusk The Fireflies Appear

At dusk the fireflies appear
As silent quasars in the dark
As gnomes with lanterns drawing near
While all around the woods loom stark.

And night doth softly settle in
The tiny signals glow and dim
And through the silhouette of leaves
Rise interlocked night's spectral trees.

And joining in the twinkling hue
The evening stars make their debut
And darkness deepening everywhere
Throbs with gold dust in the air.

Persephone

Come, sing a song of April
   Of pollen in the pine
      Of apricot and cherry bloom
         Of peach and pear and vine.

Of apple, grape, and plum tree
   So very near to blossom
      Where chickweed from the orchard path
         Hath crept into the garden.

Come, sing a song of Springtime
   Of white-faced daffodil
      Of periwinkle in the copse
         Of cedar on the hill.

And rise, Demeter, rise
   Cast off cold winter's cape
      Persephone is home again
         Your daughter's at the gate.

Against the Dark and Silent Woods

Against the dark and silent woods
The buck with lance-like antlers stood.

He could not see me in the vines
Behind the hemlock boughs and pines.

But seasoned nostril and trembling skin
Forewarned of human scent again.

And sensing danger
      From a stranger
            That he could not see,

He disappeared into the laurel
And sorrel branches of a tree.

Epitaph

Reeling russet broomsedge sheathes
Bow uniformly in the breeze.
Young pine seedlings bristle green
Behind rough rolling sorrel grass
    Swaying in the wind.

Sometimes the land I love comes back to me
    In cedar trees
    And broken gates
    By sagging barns.

I've climbed too many pastured hills
    Up winding cattle paths
    Not to know where home is.

But when I drive by desolate farms
And blackened tenant cabins
    And tracts of pine
    In briar vine
    With bramble on the fences

The sights and sounds of childhood years return
Made hallowed by the songs a granny sang
And brightened by the whining of a dog
    Waiting on a schoolboy's
    Come-home hug.

Selected Bibliography

Alexander, Hartley Burr. *The World's Rim: Great Mysteries of the North American Indians.* Mineola, NY: Dover Publications, Inc. 1999.

Awiakta, Marilou. *Selu: Seeking the Corn-Mother's Wisdom.* Golden, CO: Fulcrum Publishing. 1993.

Birch, Charles and Cobb Jr., John B. *The Liberation of Life: From the Cell to the Community.* Cambridge and New York: Cambridge University Press. 1981.

Bonfanti, Leo. *Biographies and Legends of the New England Indians.* Wakefield, Mass.: Pride Publications. 1968.

Bruchac, Joseph. *Roots of Survival: Native American Storytelling and the Sacred.* Golden, CO: Fulcrum Publishing. 1996.

Carus, Paul, comp. *The Gospel of Buddha.* New York: Open Court Publishing Company. 1894,1915.

Chuang Tsu. *Inner Chapters.* Trans. Gia-Fu Feng and Jane English. New York: Vintage Books. 1974.

Clark, Ella E. *Indian Legends from the Northern Rockies.* Norman: University of Oklahoma. 1966.

Dawood, N.J., trans. *The Koran.* Kingsport: TN: Kingsport Press, Inc. Penguin Books. 1972.

Deer, John (Fire) Lame and Erdoes, Richard. *Lame Deer: Seeker of Visions.* New York: Pocket Books. 1994.

Eastman, Charles A. *Indian Boyhood.* New York: McClure, Phillips, 1902.

Ehrlich, Paul. *The Machinery of Nature.* New York: Simon and Schuster. 1986.

Erdoes, Richard. *The Sun Dance People: The Plains Indians, Their Past and Present.* New York: Alfred A. Knopf. 1972.

Gordon, Cyrus H., trans. *Ugarit and Minoan Crete*. New York.
    NP. 1966.
Griffith, Ralph T.H., trans. *The Hymns of the Rig Veda*.
    Delhi: Motilal Banarsidas. 1976.
Grinnell, George Bird. *Pawnee Hero Stories and Folk Tales*.
    New York: Forest and Stream Publishing. 1889.
Hausman, Gerald. *Meditations With the Navajo*. Sante Fe:
    Bear & Company. 1987.
Hawking, Stephen. *A Brief History of Time: From the Big
    Bang to Black Holes*. New York: Bantam Books. 1990.
Haile, Berard. *The Upward Moving and Emergence Way*.
    Lincoln: Univertsity of Nebraska Press. 1981.
Hultkrantz, Ake. *Native Religions of North America*. San
    Francisco: Harper and Row. 1987.
Joseph, Frank. *Sacred Sites*. St. Paul: Minn.: Llewellyn
    Publications. 1992.
Josephy, Alvin M. *The Indian Heritage of America*. New
    York: Alfred A. Knopf. 1968.
Kramer, Samuel Noah. *The Sumerians: Their History,
    Culture, and Character*. Chicago. 1963.
Langdon, Stephen. *Tammuz and Ishtar*. Oxford. 1914.
Lao Tsu. *Tao Te Ching*. Trans. by Gia-Fu Feng and Jane
    English. New York: Vintage Books. 1972.
Leakey, Richard E. with Lewin, Roger. *Origins*. New York:
    E. P. Dutton. 1977.
Leopold, Aldo. *A Sand County Almanac: With Other Essays
    on Conservation*. New York: Oxford University Press.
    1966.
Linderman, Frank B. *Plenty-Coups: Chief of the Crows*.
    Lincoln: University of Nebraska Press. 1962.
Locke, Raymond Friday. *The Book of the Navajo*. Los
    Angles: Mankind Publishing Company. 1992.
Lovelock, James. *The Ages of Gaia*. Oxford: Oxford
    University Press. 1988.
McTaggart, Fred. *Wolf That I am*. Boston: Houghton Mifflin.
    1976.
Neihardt, John G. *Black Elk Speaks*. Lincoln: University of
    Nebraska Press. 1979.

Ortiz, Simon. *Woven Stone*. Tucson: University of Arizona Press. 1992.

Platt, John R. *The Steps to Man*. New York: John Wiley and Sons. 1996.

Powell, Major J.W. *The Hopi Villages: The Ancient Province of Tusayan*. Palmer Lake, CO: Filter Press. 1972.

Prabhupada, A.C.Bhaktivedanta Swami. *Bhagavad-Gita As It Is*. New York: The Bhaktivedanta Book Trust. 1972.

Prigogine, Ilya and Stenger, Isabelle. *Order Out of Chaos: Man's New DialogueWith Nature*. New York: Bantam Books. 1984.

Pritchard, James B., Editor. *The Ancient Near East: An Anthology of Texts and Pictures*. Princeton: Princeton University Press. 1953.

Reichard, Gladys A. *Navaho Religion: A Study of Symbolism*. Bollingen Series. Princeton: Princeton University Press. 1970.

Reps, Paul. Comp. *Zen Flesh, Zen Bones*. New York: Anchor Books/Doubleday. 1989.

Roscoe, Will. *The Zuni Man-Woman*. Albuquerque: University of New Mexico Press. 1991.

Scheffer, Victor B. *Spire of Form: Glimpses of Evolution*. University of Washington Press. 1983.

Seltzer, Robert M., Editor. *Religions of Antiquity*. New York: Macmillan Publishing Company. 1989.

Shibayama, Zenkei. *Zen Comments on the Mumonkan*. Trans. Sumiko Kudo. New York: New American Library. A Mentor Book. 1975.

Stone, Merlin. *Ancient Mirrors of Womanhood: Our Goddess and Heroine Heritage*. 2 vols. New York:Dorset Press. 1979.

_____. *When God Was a Woman*. New York: Dorset Press. 1976.

Suzuki, Daisetz T. *Zen and Japanese Culture*. Princeton: Princeton University Press. 1959.

Suzuki, David and Knudtson, Peter. *Wisdom of the Elders: Sacred Native Stories of Nature*. New York: Bantam Books. 1993.

Tyler, Hamilton. *Pueblo Gods and Myths*. Norman: University of Oklahoma Press. 1964.

Waters, Frank. *Book of the Hopi*. New York: Penguin Books. 1977.

Weatherford, Jack. *Indian Giver*. New York: Crown Publishing. 1988.

_____. *Native Roots*. New York: Fawcett Columbine. 1991.

Wilson, Edward O. *Biophilia*. Cambridge: Harvard University Press. 1984.

Zolbrod, Paul G. *Dine Bahane: The Navajo Creation Story*. Albuquerque: University of New Mexico Press. 1984.